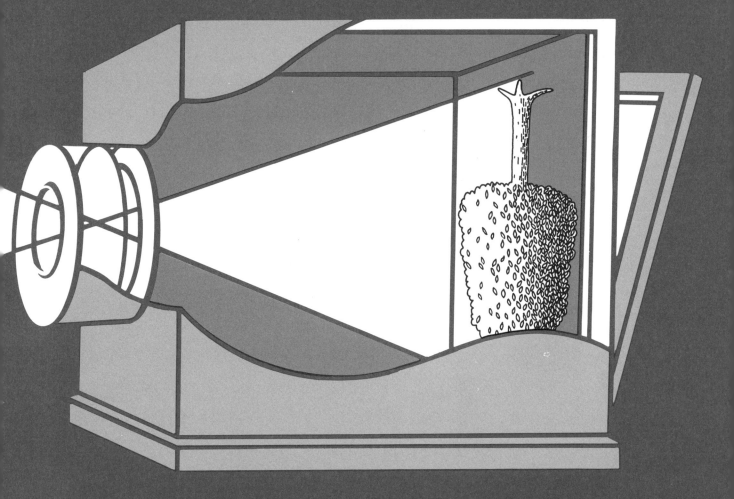

UNDERSTANDING SCIENCE & NATURE

Machines & Inventions

TIME-LIFE
ALEXANDRIA, VIRGINIA

CONTENTS

1
Inventions That Changed History

What drives inventors is the need to spare effort and to make things work better. People tried to improve their lot for millennia, first with basic inventions—making fire, simple tools, the wheel—then with more complex machines. Our world benefits from these inventions and the influence of thousands of technological advances, great and small. A few inventions were so dramatic in their impact that, in themselves, they changed the course of history.

When considering the history of technological advance, computer pioneer Norbert Wiener divided the modern era into three main periods. The first he called the Age of the Clock. The development of ever more accurate timepieces from the 14th century onward enabled the great explorers to calculate their positions with greater confidence on their voyages of discovery. Wiener's second period was the Age of the Internal-Combustion Engine. Development of a practical gasoline-powered engine dramatically increased humankind's mobility and permitted the conquest of the air. Wiener's final period is today's Age of the Computer, in which programmable calculating devices are finding application in everything from washing machines to spacecraft. Some historians of technology have emphasized other inventions that changed history, notably the printing press, gunpowder, and the steam engine. However one views the history of technological development, it is clear that humankind's creativity has profoundly changed the world in which we live.

A series of developments in science and technology have powerfully influenced the scope of human life. New inventions that will again change history are certain to be found on the road ahead.

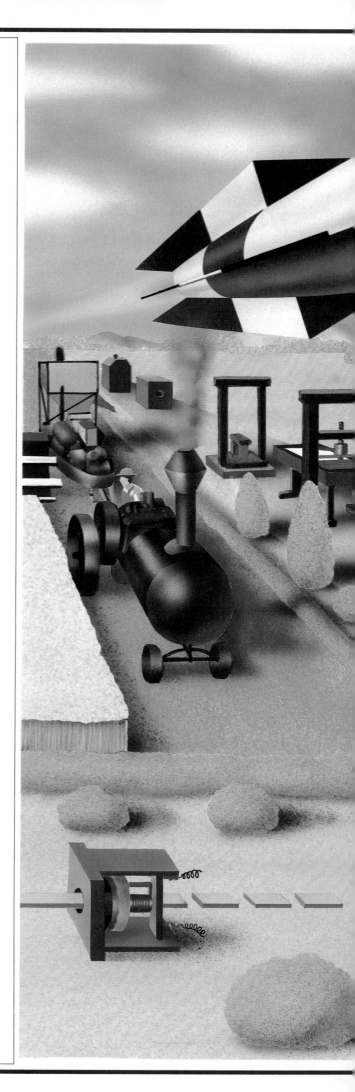

How Was the Printing Press Invented?

Before the mid-15th century, books in Europe were rare and expensive, each painstakingly copied and illustrated by hand. In China people carved wooden blocks with words and pictures, inked the blocks, and pressed them against paper. But this method was equally slow. Then a German silversmith named Johannes Gutenberg invented the first printing press using movable type. Gutenberg cast type of the individual letters of the alphabet from an alloy of lead, tin, and antimony. Once the type was cast, the letters could be arranged to form words into a complete page of text. Pressing a sheet of paper against the ink-coated type produced a full page of print. Up to 100 copies of each page were printed, then the type was recomposed to form the next page, until a complete book had been printed. The speed of the Gutenberg method meant that from then on books could easily be printed by the hundreds, with the result that knowledge, news, and opinion rapidly spread across Europe.

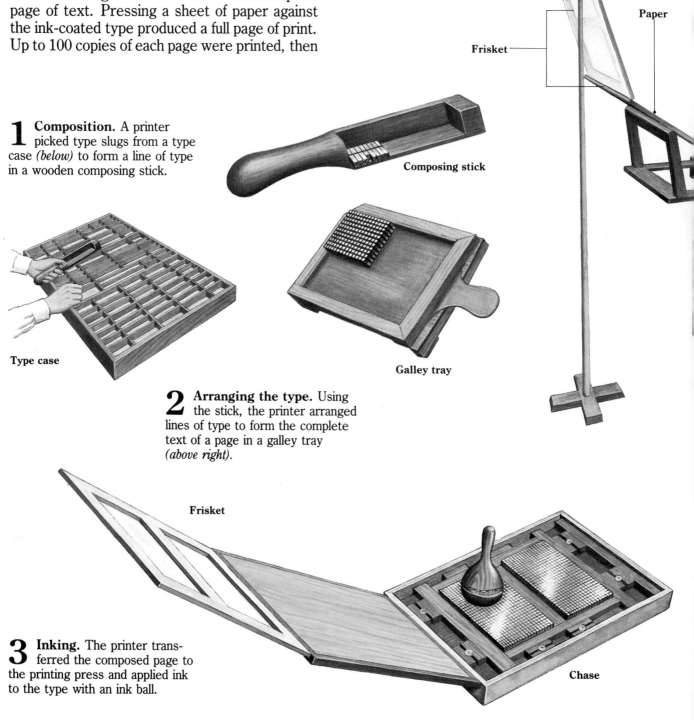

1 Composition. A printer picked type slugs from a type case *(below)* to form a line of type in a wooden composing stick.

Composing stick

Type case

Galley tray

Frisket

Paper

Frisket

2 Arranging the type. Using the stick, the printer arranged lines of type to form the complete text of a page in a galley tray *(above right).*

3 Inking. The printer transferred the composed page to the printing press and applied ink to the type with an ink ball.

Chase

The printing process

Press handle

Chase

Rail

Johannes Gutenberg (1397–1468) is credited with inventing the first European printing press with movable type in 1438. The press was an adaptation of the wine press widely in use in the vineyards near his hometown of Mainz.

Casting the type

Gutenberg cut a punch of hard metal into the shape of a type character (1) and pressed the punch into a softer metal to produce the matrix (2). He poured a melted alloy into the box (3) and let the metal harden into a type slug (4).

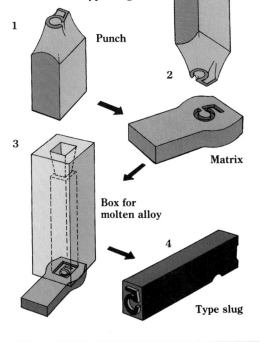

1

Punch

2

3

Matrix

Box for molten alloy

4

Type slug

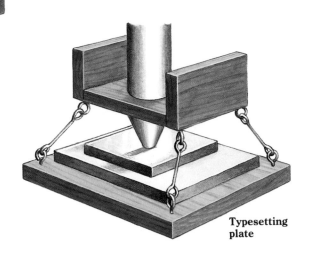

Typesetting plate

4 **Printing.** The printer placed paper over the type in the chase and held it in place with a frame. By turning the lever, he applied pressure to the plate and printed the text.

The Gutenberg Bible

The first book Gutenberg printed was a Bible set at 42 lines per page and published in 1455. The ornamental design work was still done by hand.

Who Developed the Telegraph?

In the late 18th century, scientists discovered that electrical current could be transmitted over wires across long distances almost instantly. Experiments continued into the 19th century, and by 1835 American inventor Samuel F. B. Morse had developed the first practical telegraph. Morse's device transmitted short and long bursts of current—dots and dashes—which, in various combinations, represented the letters of the alphabet and numbers. The pulses of current caused a magnet to move a pen in the telegraph receiver, recording the sequence of dots and dashes for later decoding by the operator. Relay stations allowed the signals to be carried long distances, and soon the first telegraph cable connecting England with the Continent had been laid. By 1858 the first transatlantic cable connected Ireland and Newfoundland. Although this first cable failed soon after its installation, a second cable completed in 1866 proved to be longer lasting. Suddenly, rapid communications to far-flung places were possible, and the invention of the telegraph paved the way for all electromagnetic communications to come.

Samuel F. B. Morse (1791-1872) was an artist as well as an inventor.

The Baltimore-Washington link

Embosser

Electromagnet

Paper tape

Tape transport mechanism

Morse sent the first telegraph message between Washington and Baltimore on this device in 1844.

8

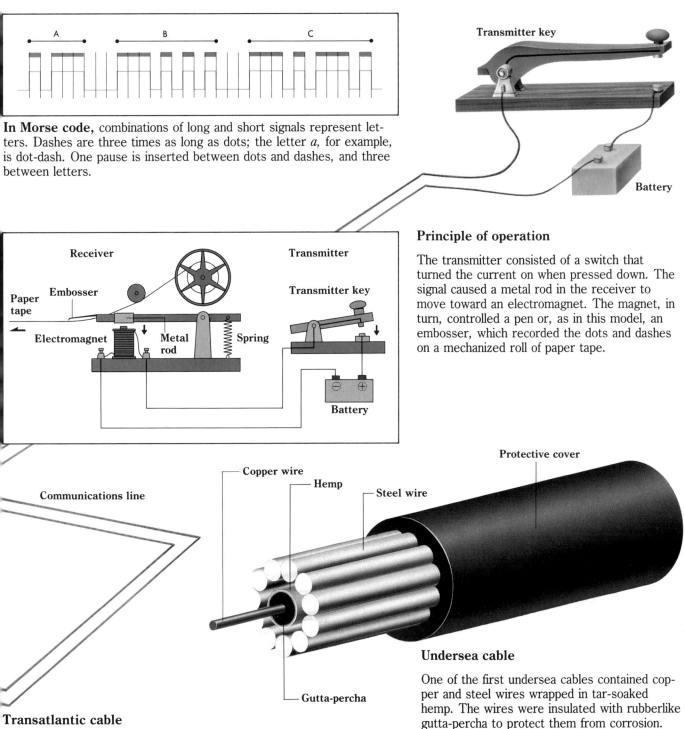

In Morse code, combinations of long and short signals represent letters. Dashes are three times as long as dots; the letter *a,* for example, is dot-dash. One pause is inserted between dots and dashes, and three between letters.

Principle of operation

The transmitter consisted of a switch that turned the current on when pressed down. The signal caused a metal rod in the receiver to move toward an electromagnet. The magnet, in turn, controlled a pen or, as in this model, an embosser, which recorded the dots and dashes on a mechanized roll of paper tape.

Undersea cable

One of the first undersea cables contained copper and steel wires wrapped in tar-soaked hemp. The wires were insulated with rubberlike gutta-percha to protect them from corrosion.

Transatlantic cable

After the failure of the first transatlantic cable, a cable linking Newfoundland and Ireland was completed in 1866, with help from American financier Cyrus W. Field and the technical creativity of British scientist William Thomson, later Lord Kelvin.

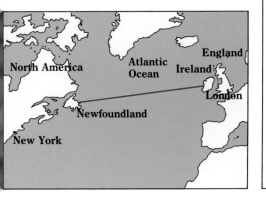

Thomson's galvanometer

Electrical signals weaken over long distances. Thomson solved this problem with his galvanometer. Each signal caused a magnetic needle to flutter. A mirror reflected lamplight onto a reading scale and amplified the flutters, which could be read as dots and dashes.

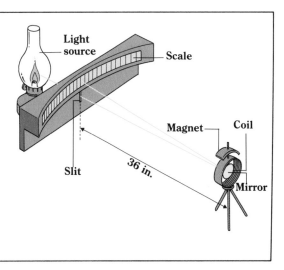

9

How Did Bell's Telephone Work?

During an experiment to determine if several different signals could be sent over the same telegraph wire, Alexander Graham Bell found that thin vibrating reeds attached to each end of the wire produced a sound. Bell then placed metallic reeds and a diaphragm membrane in front of an electromagnet in both the transmitter and the receiver, which were almost alike. As an electric current flowed through the connecting wire, the sound of someone speaking into the transmitter was reproduced by the receiver. So startling was the sound of the human voice from the receiver, it seemed like magic to listeners in 1876. But today telephones are everyday objects that allow worldwide communication.

Bell's telephone

Bell's prototype telephone, the "gallows phone" *(below)*, never worked well enough to reproduce the human voice but had all the parts of the working model. Sound waves caused the transmitter's diaphragm to vibrate, moving a reed over an electromagnet and creating fluctuations in the current. When these fluctuations reached the receiver, they caused vibrations in the diaphragm and re-created the sound.

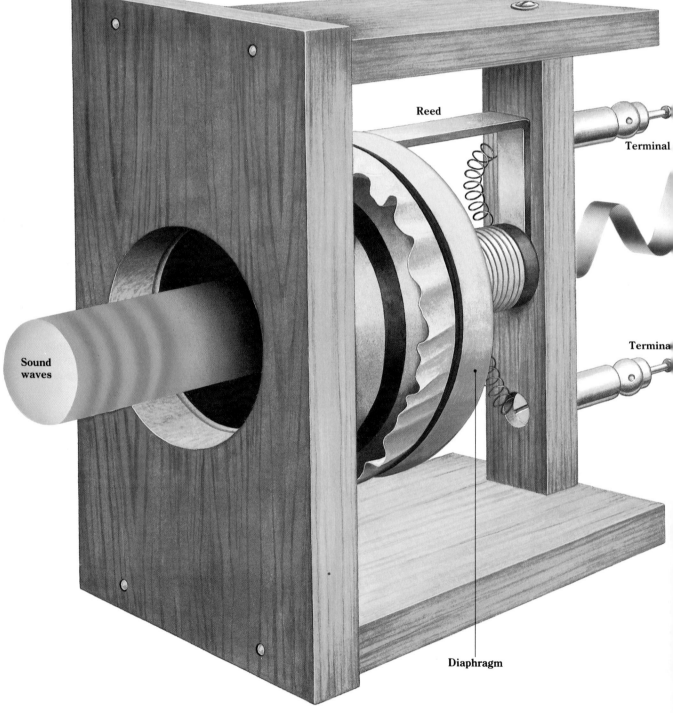

Transmitter

Reed

Terminal

Sound waves

Terminal

Diaphragm

The Bell "gallows" experiment

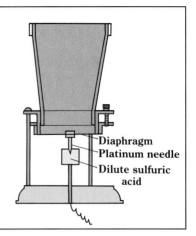
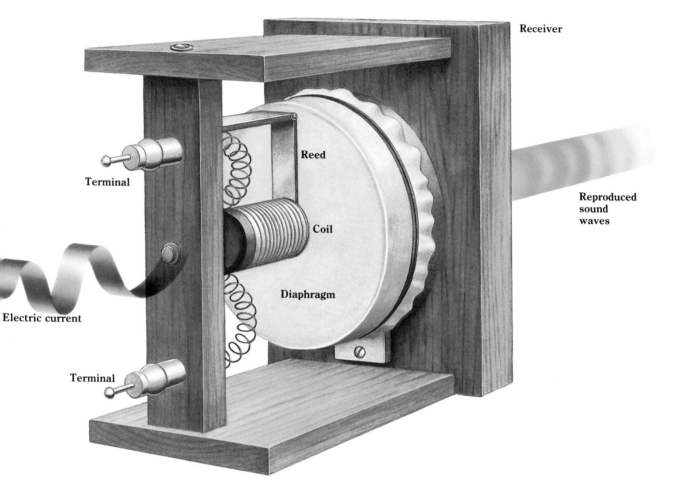

Receiver

Reed

Reproduced sound waves

Terminal

Coil

Electric current

Diaphragm

Terminal

Operating principle

This diagram shows how electric current from the battery creates electromagnetic flux in the coil. The induced current varies in response to the diaphragm's motions, which are caused by sound waves in the transmitter. The receiver's diaphragm duplicates these vibrations to reproduce the sound.

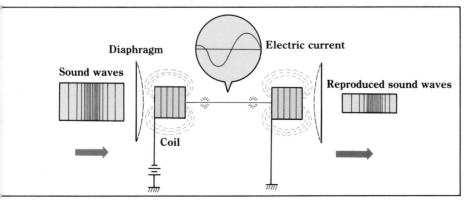

Diaphragm
Electric current
Sound waves
Reproduced sound waves
Coil

Alexander Graham Bell (1847-1922). The Scots-born Bell filed his American patent application for the telephone in 1876. Bell also researched speech therapy for the deaf and experimented with other sound equipment.

How Do Mechanical Clocks Keep Time?

For most of human history, people had little awareness of time. Although timekeepers, such as the sundial and hourglass, date back to ancient cultures, the rising and setting of the sun, moon, and stars provided as much chronological accuracy as most people needed. By the 14th century, however, technical progress prompted the creation of the first mechanical clocks, which summoned people to prayers from church steeples or rang from public buildings. The heart of the clock was the verge escapement, which caused a weighted drum to rotate at a fixed speed. The mechanism consisted of a crossbar mounted on a spindle, with weights at both ends. The crossbar moved back and forth, causing the spindle to rotate; pallets on the spindle's shaft would intermittently engage the gear teeth of the escape mechanism. This arrangement caused the drum to turn at an even pace while the hand of the clock rotated at the same rate as the pallets. The accurate measurement of time permitted the creation of a more structured society and the development of modern institutions of commerce and government.

Verge escapement mechanism

As the weights move the crossbar to and fro, pallets on opposite sides of the spindle engage the gear teeth of the escape wheel, momentarily halting the rotation of the wheel. When the crossbar reverses its motion, the pallets disengage and the wheel resumes its rotation until the next set of gear teeth engages. Falling weights keep the wheel turning at a constant rate.

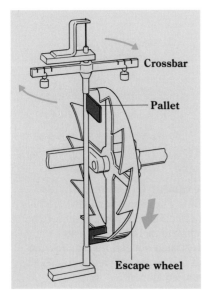

Crossbar

Pallet

Escape wheel

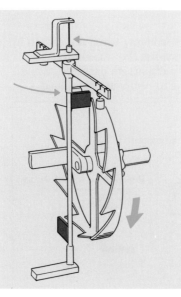

Henri de Vic's clock

Henri de Vic was engaged in 1370 by King Charles V of France to build this 10-foot-high clock, which still adorns the wall of the Supreme Court in Paris. The clock took 8 years to complete.

Transmission of motion

As the weight falls, gear 1 rotates and transmits the motion to gear 2, which causes the escape wheel (3) to move. As the rotation of gear 1, controlled by the escape mechanism, reaches gear 4, the hand of the clock turns. A clock keeper had to wind up the weight every day.

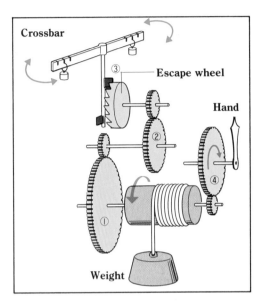

Crossbar

③ Escape wheel

Hand

②

①

④

Weight

The pendulum clock

In 1656 Dutch astronomer Christiaan Huygens applied the principle that a pendulum swings at a constant rate, regardless of the distance it moves, to perfect the pendulum clock.

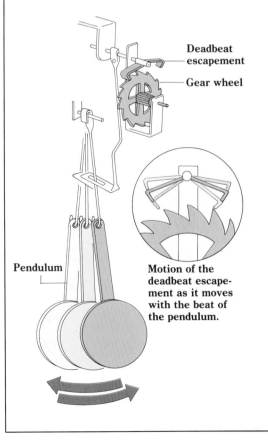

Deadbeat escapement

Gear wheel

Pendulum

Motion of the deadbeat escapement as it moves with the beat of the pendulum.

What Is a Combine?

In 19th-century Europe, small farm plots supported many people who worked the fields by hand. But in America, vast tracts of land opened up to agriculture at a time when relatively few people lived there. The solution to this problem was the mechanization of agriculture. A reaper drawn by horses or mules could do the work of several men. As mechanization progressed, the ever-improving farm equipment could perform additional tasks. In 1875 a large mechanical combine, drawn by teams of horses, was introduced. The combine not only cut the standing grain but also threshed the grain, to separate it from the straw and chaff, cleaned the grain, and discharged it into bags or bundles. Steam-powered tractors soon replaced horses and mules, but these machines proved to be heavy and awkward. By the 20th century, gasoline-powered tractors and eventually self-propelled combines came into use, speeding up the harvest in the early 1990s to 10 acres per hour. The widespread mechanization of agriculture has revolutionized the world we live in by making it possible for a small number of agricultural workers to produce enough food to feed a large and expanding urban population.

1 **Animal-drawn combine (1880s).** Pulled by as many as 24 horses, the first combines could reap and thresh about ¾ acre of wheat in an hour.

Area harvested in 1 hour: about ¾ acre.

3 **Gasoline tractor combine (1930s).** The introduction of gasoline engines increased horsepower by about 100 percent over the larger, less maneuverable steam tractor. With a gasoline tractor, 2 acres of wheat could be harvested in about 1 hour. In this type of combine, a cutter bar cut the grain stalks, which were then scooped up by a stack auger and carried on a chain conveyor belt to the thresher. There, the grain was held down to prevent spillage and separated from straw and chaff. The grain fell through a sieve as a fan blew away the chaff. The threshed grain was collected by a grain auger, while unthreshed grain was re-collected by a tailing auger and returned to the thresher. Straw was transported outside the combine to the straw rack.

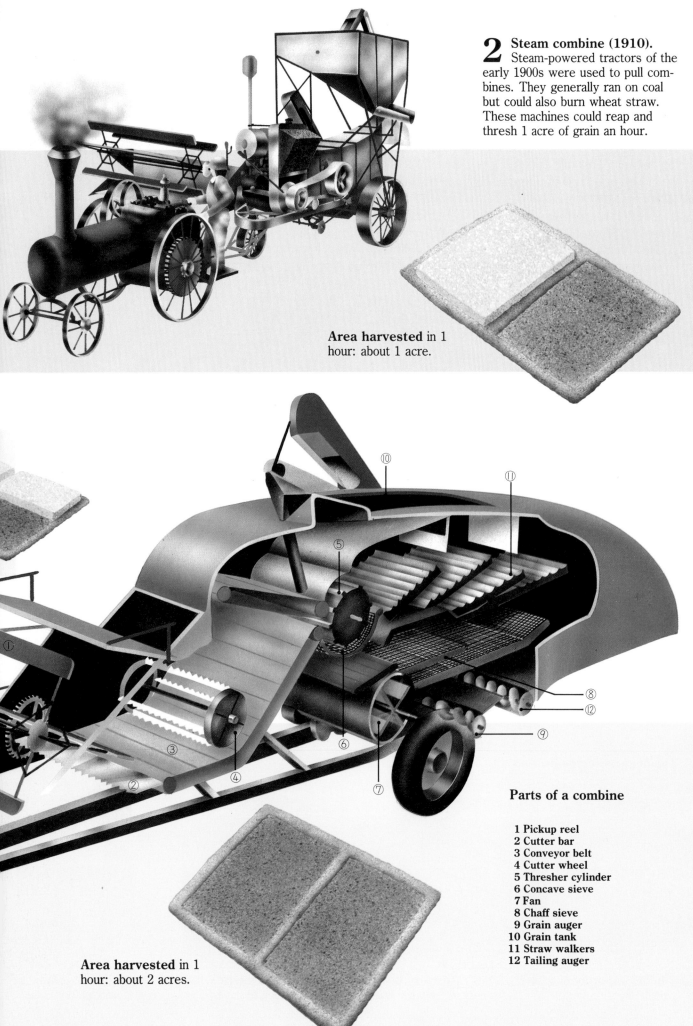

2 **Steam combine (1910).**
Steam-powered tractors of the early 1900s were used to pull combines. They generally ran on coal but could also burn wheat straw. These machines could reap and thresh 1 acre of grain an hour.

Area harvested in 1 hour: about 1 acre.

Area harvested in 1 hour: about 2 acres.

Parts of a combine

1 Pickup reel
2 Cutter bar
3 Conveyor belt
4 Cutter wheel
5 Thresher cylinder
6 Concave sieve
7 Fan
8 Chaff sieve
9 Grain auger
10 Grain tank
11 Straw walkers
12 Tailing auger

How Did the First Camera Work?

The camera obscura, literally "dark room," was a 16th-century ancestor of the modern camera. This invention worked by projecting an image through a pinhole into a darkened room, showing the scene upside down on a wall. Later the camera obscura became a box fitted with a lens that projected an inverted image onto the far wall of the box. In the 19th century, French lithographer Joseph-Nicéphore Niepce succeeded in permanently capturing an image by coating the wall with a light-sensitive asphalt. His colleague Louis Daguerre built on this work. He sensitized a silvered plate with iodine vapor, exposed the plate to light, then developed the image with mercury vapor. Daguerre and Niepce also experimented with an early form of color photography, but lasting results eluded them. The black-and-white daguerreotype, however, became popular throughout the world and led to modern black and white photography.

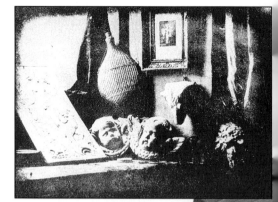

An early daguerreotype

The lens

Early daguerreotype cameras used a lens, made by French optician C. L. Chevalier, that combined concave and convex lenses.

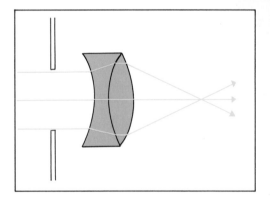

Lens aperture

The lens aperture in the diagram below is open. To close it, the photographer had to lift a pin and move the cover.

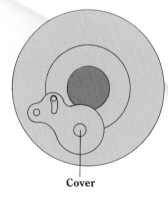

Cover

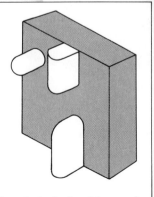

Lens

Aperture

The daguerreotype process

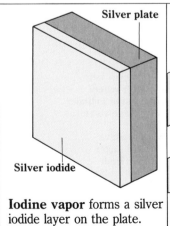

Silver plate

Silver iodide

Iodine vapor forms a silver iodide layer on the plate.

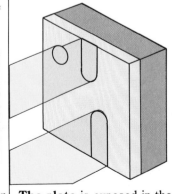

The plate is exposed in the camera to form the image.

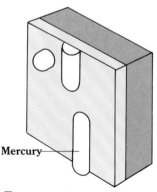

Mercury

Exposure to mercury vapor develops the image.

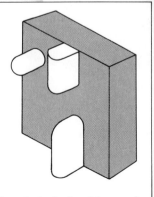

The plate is fixed by washing in a salt solution.

Daguerreotype camera

Introduced in 1839, the 15-by-12-by-20-inch camera consisted of two wooden boxes, one sliding inside the other. A lens on the outer box focused the image.

Mirror

Louis Daguerre (1789-1851) was a French studio artist. After introducing the daguerreotype camera in 1839, he sold the rights to the French government in return for a lifetime pension.

Who Invented the Box Camera?

The daguerreotype method of photography was an awkward and difficult process. Cameras had to be held steady on tripods in order to make the long exposures necessary for the "wet plate" technique. The cameras were heavy and difficult to carry. In the 1870s, "dry plate" photography was introduced, but it remained for George Eastman, an American hobbyist, to develop the means of making photography a practical and truly popular pastime. In 1888 Eastman introduced his Kodak box camera. Instead of wet or dry plates, the Kodak used a 100-image strip of roll film, which was initially made of photosensitive paper but was soon replaced by coated transparent celluloid. Once the roll of film was exposed, the user shipped the entire camera to Eastman's factory in Rochester, N.Y. There, technicians developed the pictures and shipped the camera and a new roll of film back to the customer. With these basic procedures Eastman established the photographic industry. Eastman made taking pictures easy, advertising his system with the popular slogan "You press the button, we do the rest."

Selling a new hobby

Eastman transformed photography into a pastime. Ads such as this assured the public that photography was so simple everyone could do it; nearly everyone did.

The Kodak camera

Reels

Film surface

Shutter

The Kodak box camera, introduced in 1888, could be held in both hands. The focus was fixed for objects beyond 8 feet.

Lens

19th-century photography

Before the Kodak camera, photography was complex and required a lot of equipment and expertise. Venturing beyond the studio meant loading a wagon with the camera, tripod, photo-processing chemicals, a tent to use as a darkroom, numerous accessories, and, usually, a photographer's assistant.

● The development of roll film

The first roll film for the Kodak had a paper base. Photographs taken with the film tended to yellow. The paper film was soon replaced by silicate-coated celluloid, with a light-sensitive gelatin. This process created permanent negative images that could be developed more easily. Roll film soon led to the development of motion-picture cameras.

George Eastman (1854-1932) was a New York bank employee who took up photography as a hobby. After a photo expedition at the age of 23, he devoted himself to finding an easier way of taking photographs.

Portrait of the inventor: In 1890 Eastman poses on a ship with his Kodak.

Eastman's photographic system

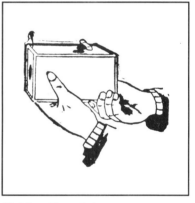

Taking the picture was a snap. The photographer simply aimed the camera and pressed a button.

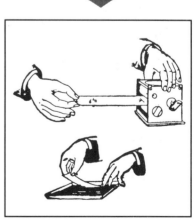

The photographer sent the camera, and $10, to the Eastman Company for developing.

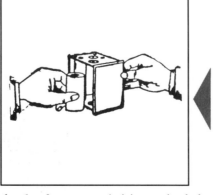

At the factory technicians reloaded the camera and returned the developed photos and camera.

What Is a Kinetoscope?

A movie consists of a series of still photographs, taken in rapid succession. The position of objects in the photographs changes very slightly from one picture, or frame, to the next. Because there are limits on how fast the human eye-brain system can process incoming information, people perceive movies as continuous motion, rather than as a series of motionless frames. The development of celluloid roll film in 1888 made it possible to take photographs rapidly enough to take advantage of this phenomenon and create

"moving pictures," or movies. Thomas Edison developed the first practical motion-picture camera, known as the kinetograph, and projector, the kinetoscope. The kinetoscope was viewed by a single person as an electric light bulb illuminated a strip of film running beneath an eyepiece with a lens. Kinetoscope parlors rapidly became popular throughout the world, as people flocked to see the first moving pictures. The success of the kinetoscope soon led to the development of the movie projection system we know today.

The kinetograph

Edison developed the kinetograph—the camera—and the kinetoscope—the viewer—with his assistant, W. K. L. Dickson. The kinetograph, relatively bulky and enclosed in a wood cabinet, used film that was 35 mm in width. Edison shot his movies in a specially designed studio that rotated on tracks to follow the sun. His studio was in New Jersey, but the movie industry soon moved to California, where sunshine was more reliable.

Edison recorded the first one-minute film strips, such as "The Kiss" (above), in 1894.

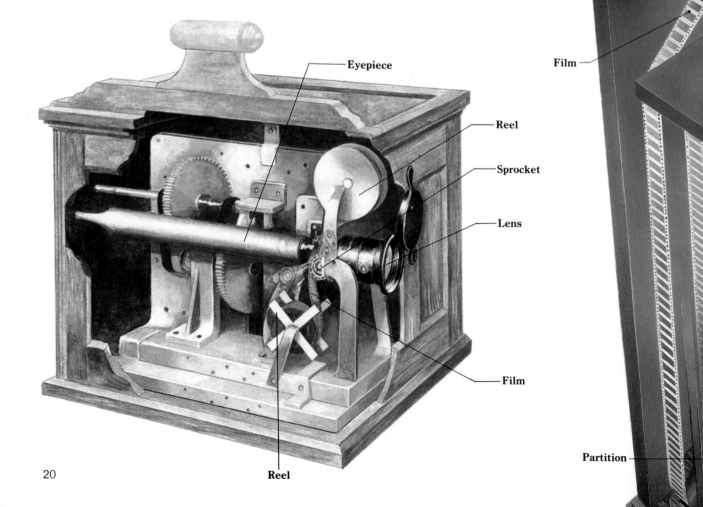

Eyepiece

Reel

Sprocket

Lens

Film

Reel

Film

Partition

The kinetoscope. Coin-operated viewing instruments showed the first silent movies. Edison made square perforations along both edges of the film to engage the sprockets in the projector. Each frame moved to a precise position, keeping the image from blurring or fluttering. The film advanced at a rate of 24 or more frames per second, producing the illusion of continuous motion.

Eyepiece

Sprockets

Light bulb

Disk

Slit

Support

The mechanism

The kinetoscope employed a rapidly spinning disk placed between the film and the light bulb. The disk had a slit about .2 inch wide, and the film was illuminated only when the slit, the film frame, and the light bulb were in vertical alignment. The disk was coupled to the sprockets so that every frame was illuminated at the same position.

Coin mechanism

Motor

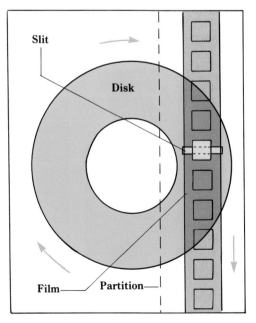

Slit

Disk

Film — Partition

What Was Early Television Like?

Television cannot be said to have had a single inventor. Rather, television was developed through a series of inventions over a span of about 50 years. In 1884 German inventor Paul Nipkow developed an optomechanical scanning disk that allowed an image to be converted in sequence to electrical signals of varying strength. Using Nipkow's disk, Scotsman John L. Baird built a practical mechanical scanning television in 1926. But mechanical scanning was limited, and the future belonged to electron scanning, which scanned across an image from left to right to divide it into a series of tiny picture elements of bright or dark dots, called pixels. The breakthrough in that area came in the late 1920s when American inventor Philo Farnsworth and Russian-American Vladimir K. Zworykin developed electron-scanning tubes. The first electronic television set received its pictures from such an iconoscope, projecting the scanned images onto a cathode-ray tube—a glass vacuum tube with a screen that was coated with a phosphorescent powder. When the tube's cathode emitted a stream of electrons, the screen glowed.

Baird's televisor

John L. Baird's device used 30 scanning lines to create the crude image that was first broadcast in the late 1920s. In 1928 he sent TV signals from England to the U.S.

Resistance control knob

Resistor

Mechanical scanning television

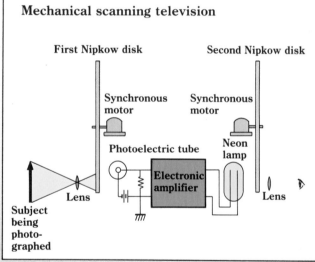

First Nipkow disk

Second Nipkow disk

Synchronous motor

Synchronous motor

Photoelectric tube

Neon lamp

Electronic amplifier

Lens

Lens

Subject being photographed

Light from the object being televised passed through a spiral of tiny holes in the Nipkow scanning disk, which rotated in front of a photoelectric tube. This produced a fluctuating electric signal that was passed to the receiver. The receiver, in turn, amplified the signal, passing the light through an identical rotating disk. As the signals changed in strength, the lines traced by the scanning disk re-created a likeness of the original object.

● **1923**

V. K. Zworykin filed a patent for the first iconoscope camera tube.

● **The RCA Victor model**

The first RCA sets had screens that faced the ceiling. Viewers saw the screen's images in a mirror. The screen consisted of a glass tube, or cathode-ray tube, coated with a photosensitive material that glowed when electrons struck it. An electron beam transmitted electric charges that changed depending on the scanned images from the camera and caused the same images to appear on the receiver screen.

● **1926**

John L. Baird developed the mechanical scanning televisor.

● **1929**

The British Broadcasting Corporation made the world's first experimental television broadcast.

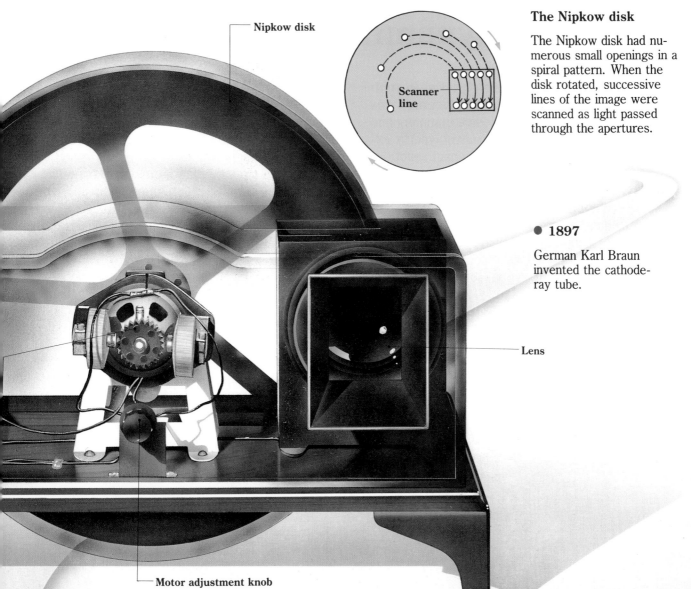

Nipkow disk

The Nipkow disk

The Nipkow disk had numerous small openings in a spiral pattern. When the disk rotated, successive lines of the image were scanned as light passed through the apertures.

Scanner line

● **1897**

German Karl Braun invented the cathode-ray tube.

Lens

Motor adjustment knob

ynchronous motor

The iconoscope

Zworykin's TV camera had a metal disk coated with light-sensing elements in the center of a glass tube. When illuminated, these elements generated current in proportion to the light's brightness. A scanner re-created the picture at the receiver.

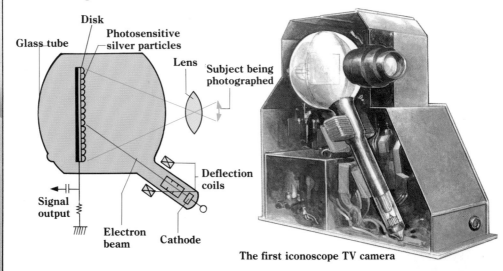

Disk

Photosensitive silver particles

Glass tube

Lens

Subject being photographed

Deflection coils

Signal output

Electron beam

Cathode

The first iconoscope TV camera

● **1930**

Philo Farnsworth developed a new scanning system that made TV suitable for home use.

How Does Dynamite Work?

In the mid-19th century, nitroglycerin—a mixture of nitric and sulfuric acids and glycerin—was the most commonly used explosive in mining and other blasting operations. In a nitroglycerin explosion, heat sets off a chemical chain reaction. This reaction rapidly increases the volume of the gases released by a thousandfold with the power to split rock apart. But nitroglycerin is very dangerous to handle and can explode if jarred even slightly. Swedish chemist Alfred Nobel, who ran a nitroglycerin factory, lost a member of his family in one such accident. Nobel set out to develop a safer, more practical explosive. He mixed nitroglycerin with a porous, absorbent earthlike material called *kieselguhr,* or diatomite, to produce a dry, granular substance. The explosive power of the product, which Nobel called dynamite, was equal to that of nitroglycerin alone, but it could be handled much more safely and was resistant to shock and heat. Another Nobel invention, the blasting cap, allowed for even safer explosions of dynamite. The invention found wide application and made a fortune for Nobel, part of which he used to establish the Nobel Prize.

Dynamite blasting cap

A conductor wire conveys electricity to a primer charge in the blasting cap, which explodes and in turn detonates the dynamite. Blasting caps provide greater safety and precision than burning fuses.

Conductor wire

Blasting cap body

Blasting cap igniter

Primer charge

Carbon dioxide

Water vapor

Nitrogen

Nitroglycerin

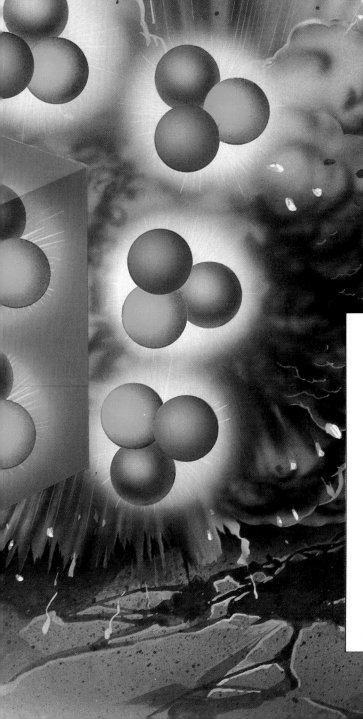

Dynamite's explosive force

When nitroglycerin explodes, water vapor, nitrogen, and carbon dioxide gases are released. The high heat of the reaction—about 9,000° F.—causes the gases to expand rapidly to more than a thousand times their original volume at room temperature, resulting in a powerful destructive force. If a high content of nitro-glycerin is used in the explosion, as in rock blasting, the reaction exerts a pressure of nearly one million pounds per square inch and creates a supersonic shock, or detonation wave, that travels at a rate of several thousand feet per second. This detonation wave exerts a severe shattering effect on anything in its path. Once the detonation wave has started, it cannot be stopped.

What Was the V-2 Rocket?

One of mankind's most ancient dreams is to explore other worlds. Early in this century, men like the Russian Konstantin Tsiolkovsky and American Robert H. Goddard began developing rocket technology that would allow the dream to become reality. After many trials a team of German scientists, the Society for Space Travel, led by Wernher von Braun, produced a first functional rocket. But the German military took over this first rocket, called the V-2, and used it instead to bombard England during World War II. The V-2 lifted off vertically and tilted to a 45° angle to fly toward its target. Its inertial guidance system relied on a preprogrammed gyropilot to keep it on course. The engine fired for about a minute, accelerating the vehicle to 4,500 feet per second. Then the engine shut off and the warhead continued on an unpowered ballistic trajectory, like a thrown stone. After the war, the rocket was further developed in the U.S. to serve in its space program.

Wernher von Braun (1912-1977) led the German rocket team and later helped plan America's Apollo missions.

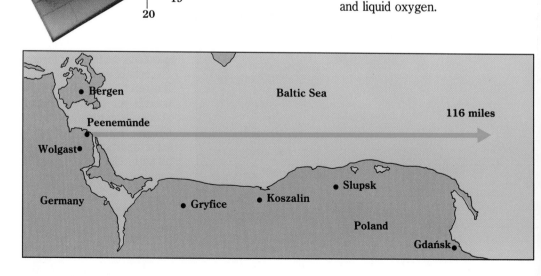

The V-2 rocket was 47 feet long and 65 inches in diameter. It weighed about 14 tons and was fueled by a mixture of ethyl alcohol and liquid oxygen.

The first flight

In 1942 the V-2 made its first successful test flight from Peenemünde, Germany, across the Baltic Sea. In 5 minutes, it traveled a distance of 116 miles and reached a maximum altitude of about 50 miles.

The V-2 rocket

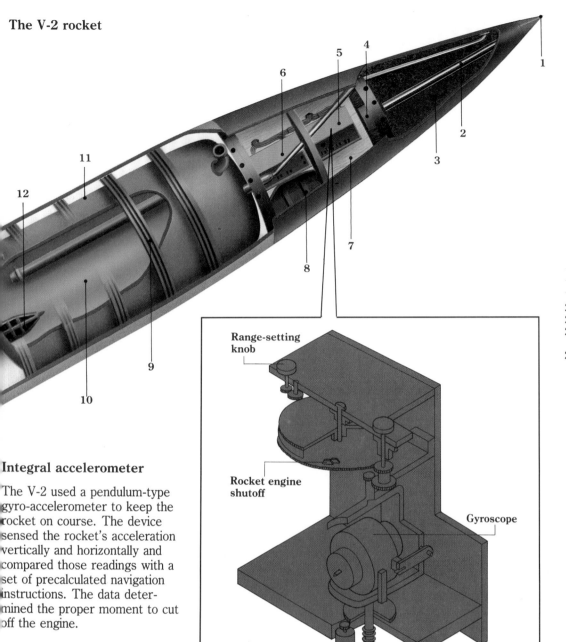

1 Warhead detonator
2 Detonator conduit
3 Warhead
4 Main electrical detonator
5 Guidance system chamber
6 Radio equipment
7 Plywood partition
8 Nitrogen tank
9 Curved ribs
10 Ethyl alcohol and water tanks
11 Glass-wool insulation
12 Control valve
13 Liquid oxygen tank
14 Insulated ethyl alcohol supply tube
15 Propulsion support frame
16 Turbopump
17 Turbine exhaust
18 Valve
19 Fuel line
20 Combustion chamber
21 Main fuel valve
22 Graphite exhaust rudder (4)
23 Movable aileron (4)

Integral accelerometer

The V-2 used a pendulum-type gyro-accelerometer to keep the rocket on course. The device sensed the rocket's acceleration vertically and horizontally and compared those readings with a set of precalculated navigation instructions. The data determined the proper moment to cut off the engine.

Range-setting knob

Rocket engine shutoff

Gyroscope

Slip ring

Automatic guidance system

The V-2's jet vanes redirected the rocket's exhaust to conform with guidance instructions from the two gyrocompasses.

Pitch → Integrator → Amplifier → II / IV

Roll → Integrator

Yaw → Integrator

Amplifier → I / III

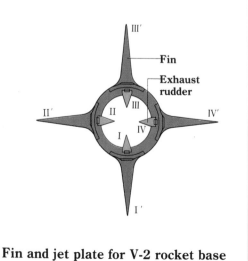

Fin

Exhaust rudder

Fin and jet plate for V-2 rocket base

How Do Electrical Generators Work?

The first electrical generator was built by Michael Faraday in Britain in 1831. Faraday had discovered that electric current is generated when a wire coil moves through the field of a magnet. If a magnet is brought near a coil, an electric current will flow through the wire; if the magnet is pulled away, the current will flow in the opposite direction. Current continues to flow as long as the magnetic field is kept in motion. Using this principle, Faraday built a device that generated current via a rotating coil attached to a magnet. His ideas were put into practice by Hippolyte Pixii of France the following year. Pixii's machine generated current by manually rotating a magnet near a stationary wire coil. Improvements to this basic design were introduced by Werner von Siemens, Zénobe-Théophile Gramme, and Thomas Edison, resulting in generators similar to those in use today. But not until the 1880s could these new designs be used for electric lighting. Since those days, the use of electricity has brought on far-reaching changes, powering everyday objects from toasters to televisions, from lights to laser beams.

In Pixii's generator, a horseshoe magnet was manually rotated beneath two coils. With each half-turn, the induced electric current cut across the magnetic lines of force, then reversed to flow in the opposite direction, producing alternating current, or AC. By installing a commutator consisting of segments of copper, Pixii switched the leads to the wires, producing a current that flowed in only one direction, or DC.

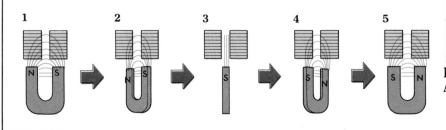

The Pixii generator

Coils

Rotating magnet

Commutator

Gearwheel

Handle

Electromagnetic induction

Pixii's machine produced electricity as shown below: (1) When coils are aligned with the magnet's poles, flux is at maximum. (2) When only partially aligned, flux decreases. (3) When not aligned, flux is zero. (4) When partially aligned again, flux is reversed but increases in the opposite direction. (5) When lined up again, flux is at maximum in the opposite direction.

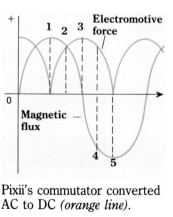

Electromotive force

Magnetic flux

Pixii's commutator converted AC to DC (*orange line*).

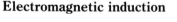

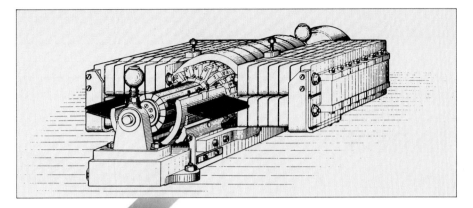

In 1856 the German Werner von Siemens introduced an improved generator featuring an armature wrapped with a bobbin-shaped coil. By 1881 a Siemens generator was being used to power a train. In 1886 he devised the first generator employing an electromagnet in place of a permanent magnet.

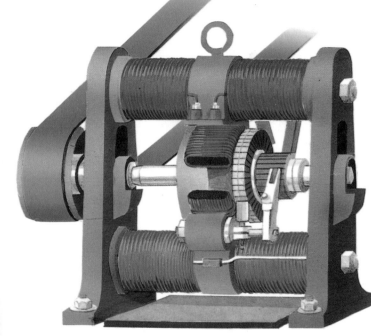

Gramme's generator

The Belgian Zénobe-Théophile Gramme solved a major problem that had plagued early generators. Coils tended to overheat and had to be cooled by water. Gramme prevented overheating with a ring-shaped coil *(above)* and the use of a steam engine to drive the generator. When Gramme's generator was introduced at an exhibition in Vienna in 1873, the generator accidentally drew current from nearby generators and began to rotate like a motor. This accident helped lead to the development of the electric motor.

Edison's generator

Thomas Edison's incandescent lights required a constant voltage, but the current output of the Siemens and Gramme generators tended to fluctuate. Edison solved the problem by building a generator consisting of two large poles with the coil positioned between and below two large electromagnets *(right)*. Edison's generator produced constant voltage as long as the rotation remained at the same rate.

2

The Machines of Industry and Science

Modern industry depends on the sophistication and reliability of its machines. Without them, the industrial world would grind to a halt. Already in the 19th century, machines such as automated looms, trains, and steam-driven ships sped work and transport. Today's machines have further extended human beings' reach and perception. Linked often with integrated-circuit electronics, advanced instruments can peer into realms inaccessible to the naked eye and can detect sounds, motions, and odors that are too faint to register on the senses.

These new machines and instruments have often been developed under highly specialized circumstances for industry, science, or space exploration. Many of these machines remain confined to factories or laboratories, because they are too expensive and delicate to be in wide service. But a few, such as speed guns and metal detectors, are finding their way into everyday use. In the future, machines will become even more sophisticated. Computer-driven robots, for example, which are able to see and move electronically and possibly even learn, may take over hazardous or complex jobs that previously only humans could perform. This chapter examines some inventions and their role in industry and science.

Every instrument is only as good as its engineering. At right, a draftsperson produces drawings of an assortment of modern tools that are used in science and industry.

How Do Electron Microscopes Work?

Revealing details too small to be seen by the naked eye, a standard microscope uses beams of light to magnify objects up to 2,000 times. The more powerful transmission and scanning electron microscopes employ beams of electrons, the negatively charged particles found in most atoms, to magnify matter millions of times. In these microscopes, a beam of electrons is accelerated by an electric field and focused by a magnetic field. The beam's strength determines the level of magnification. The most powerful electron microscopes reveal details at the atomic level, down to about .3 nanometer, or .0000000118 inch, allowing scientists to probe the basic structure of molecules, minerals, and metals.

Magnifying with electrons

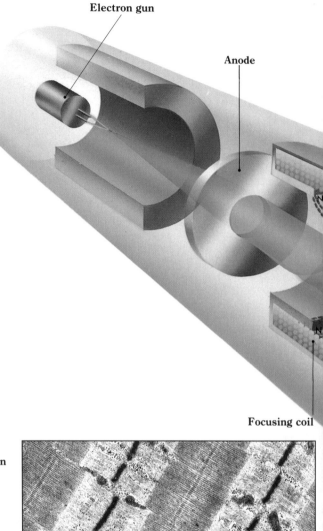

Electron gun

Anode

Focusing coil

A transmission microscope

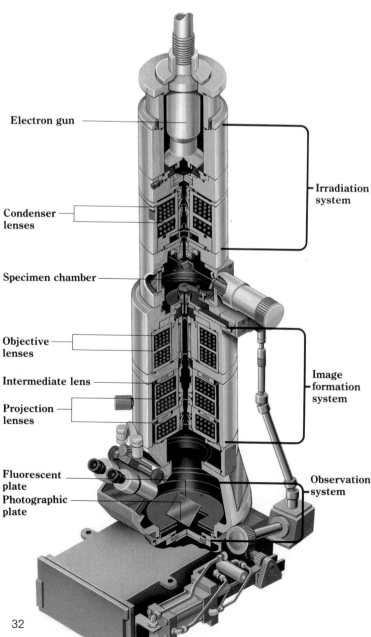

Electron gun

Condenser lenses

Specimen chamber

Objective lenses

Intermediate lens

Projection lenses

Fluorescent plate

Photographic plate

Irradiation system

Image formation system

Observation system

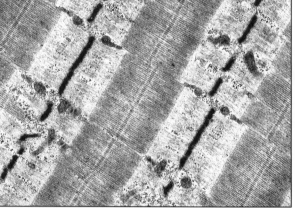

Enlarged 13,000 times, bone shows a banded structure.

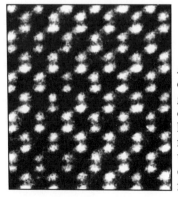

A transmission microscope yields photographic or video images of a tiny area. At left, silicon atoms, magnified two million times, line up like soldiers on parade, to form a crystal.

A scanning microscope

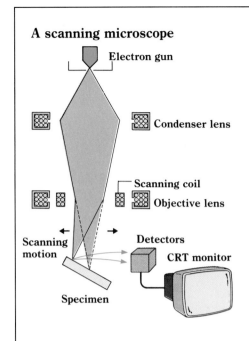

A scanning microscope systematically moves the electron beam over an entire specimen. As the beam of electrons passes over a section, atoms in the specimen also release electrons that strike a detector, causing it to emit flashes of light. These flashes are turned into electrical patterns by a photomultiplier tube and fed to a TV monitor to show a surface image of the specimen.

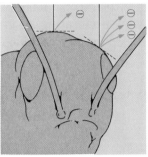

As a beam hits parts of a specimen, different numbers of electrons are released. These account for the 3-D image on the monitor.

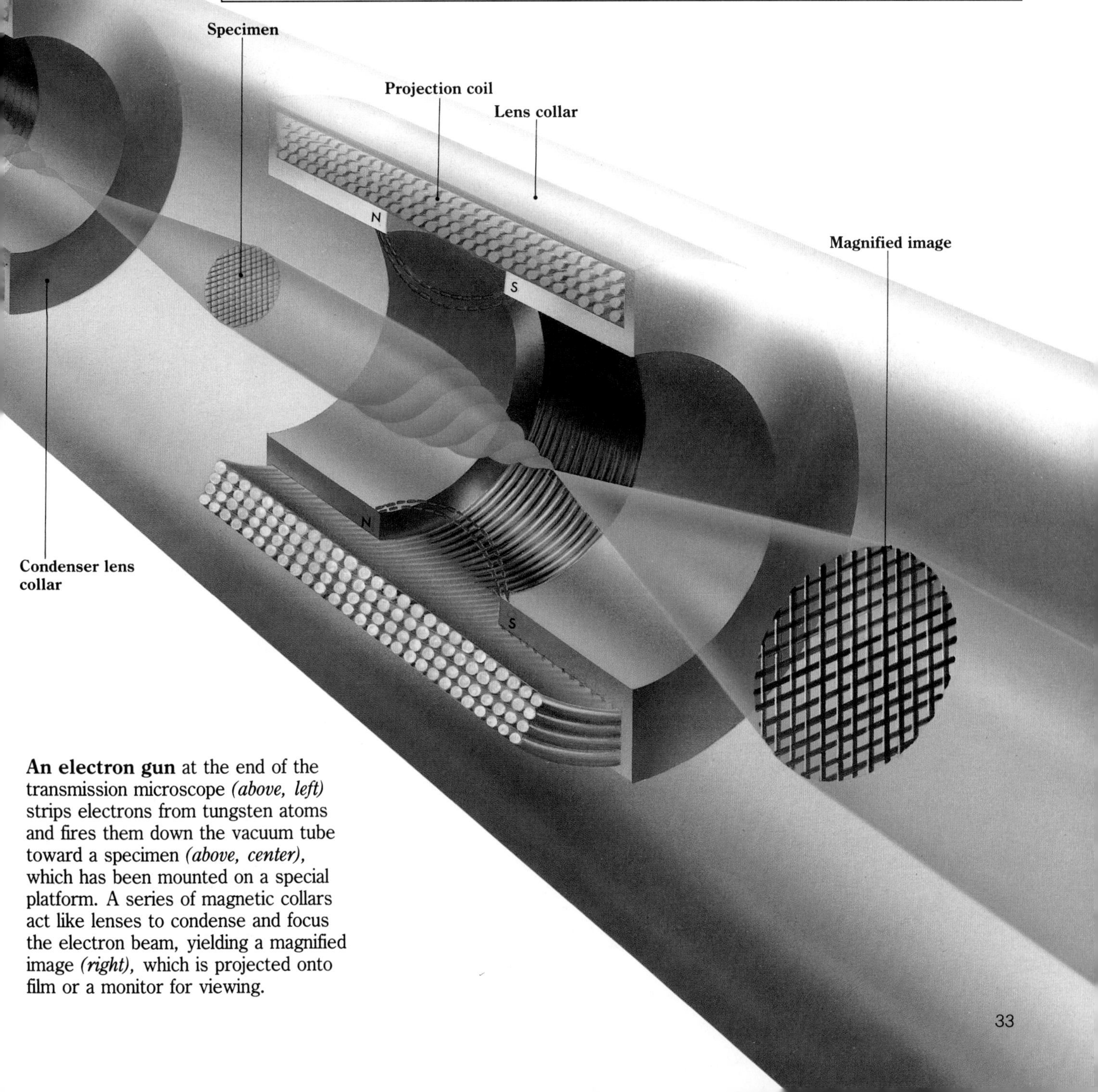

Specimen

Projection coil

Lens collar

Magnified image

Condenser lens collar

An electron gun at the end of the transmission microscope *(above, left)* strips electrons from tungsten atoms and fires them down the vacuum tube toward a specimen *(above, center),* which has been mounted on a special platform. A series of magnetic collars act like lenses to condense and focus the electron beam, yielding a magnified image *(right),* which is projected onto film or a monitor for viewing.

What Is a Sound Spectrograph?

A sound spectrograph builds a portrait of spoken words in several steps, translating the vibrations of sound waves into a series of patterns called a sound spectrogram. The conversion process begins when a subject speaks into a microphone, and his or her voice is amplified. The signal then passes through a series of electronic filters that are attuned to sound waves vibrating at given frequencies. The filters feed the analyzed signals onward to a magnetic disk, which stores a sequence about two seconds long.

This sequence is replayed over and over and dictates the up-and-down movements of a needle that tracks across a chart fastened to a spinning drum. After many revolutions of the drum, a pattern emerges, revealing the frequency and intensity of the sound waves that make up the recorded voice sequence.

A machine that charts sounds

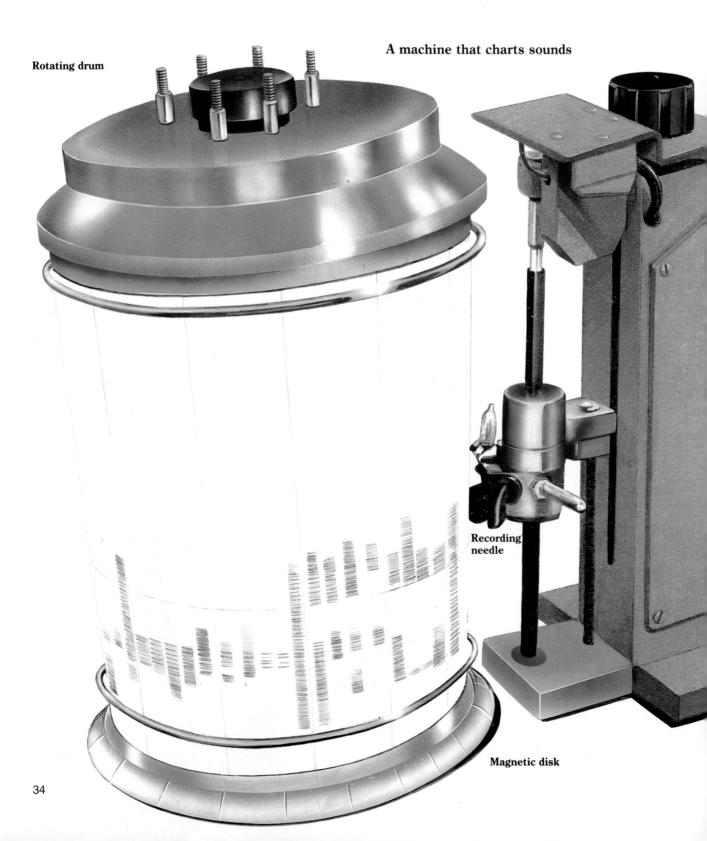

Rotating drum

Recording needle

Magnetic disk

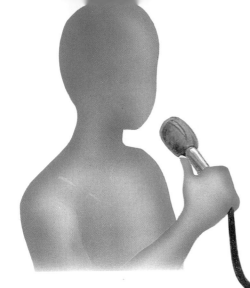

Several linked components are part of a spectrograph, including an amplifier unit *(below)*, a series of electrical filters, and a setup for recording, replaying, and graphing a person's voice.

Speaking into the mike

A person's voice passes through a microphone into the amplifier *(right)*.

Analyzer/controller

Smart circuits

Filters *(far right)* sense sound waves vibrating at 0 to 8,000 hertz, or cycles per second, and group them by frequency.

Dividing the waves

Grouping sound waves into bands either 45 or 300 hertz wide, a second circuit *(near right)* sends an analyzed signal to the magnetic disk.

Frequency signals

8000Hz

100Hz

Recording circuitry

Needle and film

Sliding on a spindle, the needle creates marks on electrically sensitive film *(left)*. The resulting track shows changes in frequency and strength.

Analytical filter

Voiceprints, like fingerprints

These color sound spectrograms were produced by the more sophisticated computerized voice spectrograph, which records the voice digitally, then analyzes it. The images map the phrase "How do you do?" as spoken by an American *(top)* and a Japanese *(bottom)* test subject. Intensity is indicated by a range of colors, with red the strongest, followed by yellow, green, light blue, blue, and violet. Because every person's voice pattern differs, such high-quality sound spectrograms, also called voiceprints, can be used for identification.

How Can Lie Detectors Spot Lies?

When a person speaks, his or her heartbeat and breathing may involuntarily quicken, and blood pressure can rise. In addition, the person's palms may perspire. The polygraph machine, also called a lie detector, monitors such physiological fluctuations as a person answers questions asked by a trained specialist. Generally, the technician asks a series of control questions first, in order to establish a subject's normal reactions, then moves to more stressful queries. If someone is psychologically shaky, as when a person is lying, the polygraph's tiny electrodes detect this. Although especially steely subjects can thwart the machine, the polygraph is used in some cases by police and other investigators who are attempting to establish the truth.

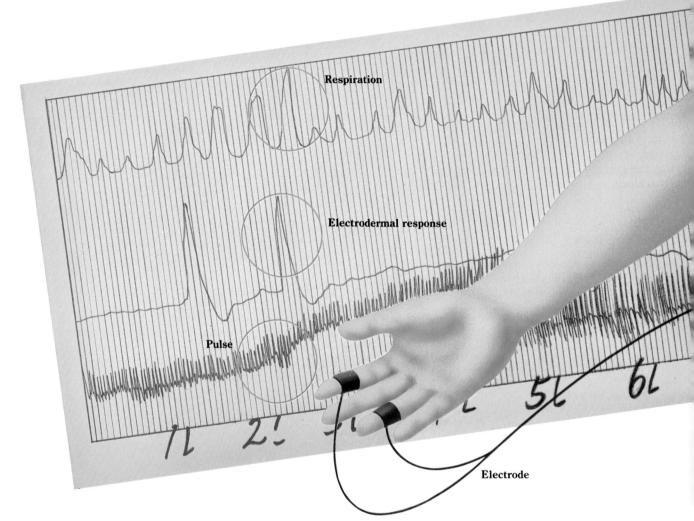

Respiration

Electrodermal response

Pulse

Electrode

How to tell a lie

Unusual patterns in the regularity of depth of a person's breathing, as revealed in the circled area *(above, top),* can indicate tension and possible lies.

A calm person shows a constant electrodermal response, or reaction in electrical properties of the skin, but with a lie *(above, middle),* it can fluctuate.

Stress often causes blood vessels to contract, elevating blood pressure and heart rate. This effect can appear as a rise in the pulse wave *(above, bottom).*

The telltale skin

Sweat glands also respond to stress, releasing perspiration that cools the body and provokes a measurable shift in the electrical conductivity of the skin. Because the most responsive glands are on the hands and soles of the feet, technicians attach electrodes there.

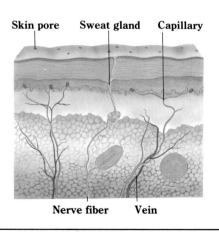

Skin pore   Sweat gland   Capillary

Nerve fiber   Vein

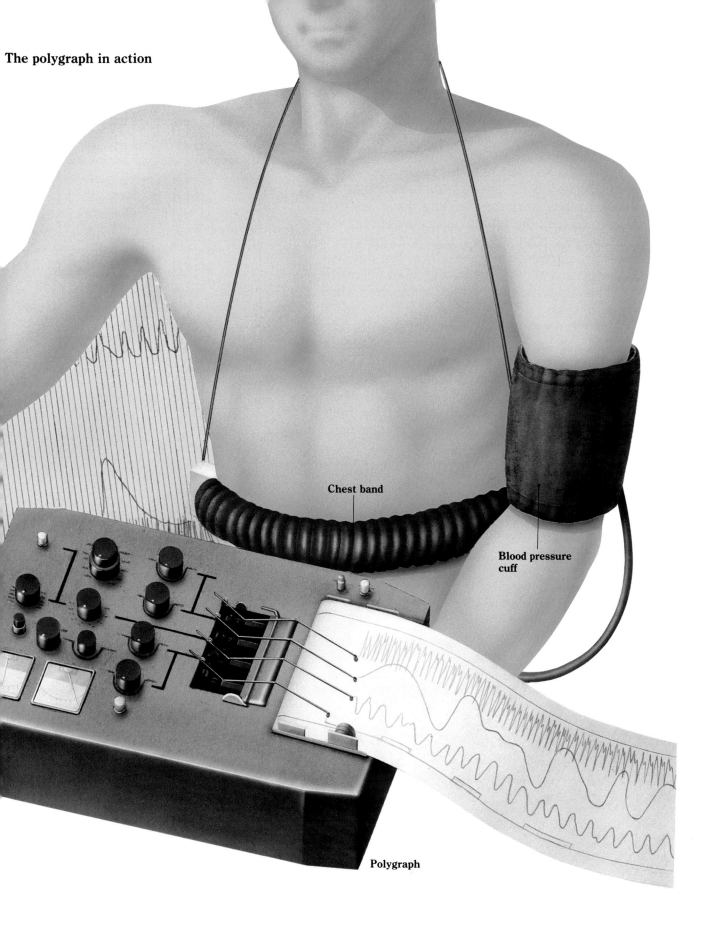

The polygraph in action

Chest band

Blood pressure cuff

Polygraph

A subject takes a polygraph examination wearing a chest band that expands and contracts as he or she breathes, a blood pressure cuff, and electrodes on the fingers. Readings from these devices flow to pens in the polygraph machine *(above)*, which produce continuous wave patterns charting respiration rate, pulse rate, and electrodermal response, a gauge of electrical properties in the skin. When a person is nervous, this reaction can show up as spikes in the waves, as on the readout above left. Trained specialists learn to identify those patterns that suggest the subject may be lying.

How Do Speed Guns Clock Baseballs?

A speed gun calculates the velocity of a baseball pitch by monitoring the Doppler shift of microwaves bounced off the ball as it flies through the air. Named after the Austrian physicist who first described the effect in 1842, the Doppler shift occurs when the distance between an observer and a moving source emitting wave motions changes over time. If the source moves toward the observer, the perceived frequency of the waves goes up; if it moves away, the frequency goes down. For this reason the steady sound of an automobile horn seems to rise in pitch as the vehicle approaches and to drop when the vehicle passes.

Armed with a receiver and a small computer-like circuit, a speed gun analyzes the interference patterns produced when the microwaves going to the baseball meet waves bouncing back from it. From this interference pattern, the computer calculates the Doppler shift and so the ball's speed. Radar guns used by traffic police operate in a similar fashion.

Reading interference patterns

Waves bounced off balls traveling at different speeds produce unique interference patterns.

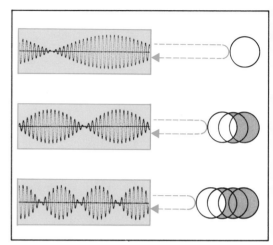

A hand-held speed gun

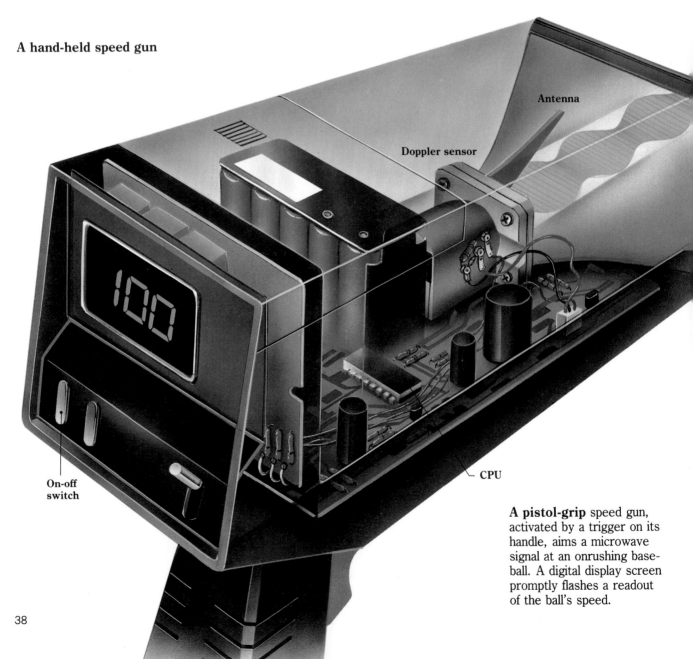

On-off switch

Doppler sensor

Antenna

CPU

A pistol-grip speed gun, activated by a trigger on its handle, aims a microwave signal at an onrushing baseball. A digital display screen promptly flashes a readout of the ball's speed.

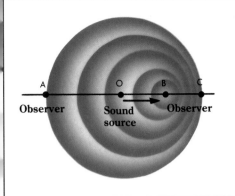

Doppler effect

To an observer at point A, the frequency of a wave moving from O to B appears lower than to the observer at point C. This effect occurs with all types of waves, including light and sound.

Interference wave

How the circuitry works

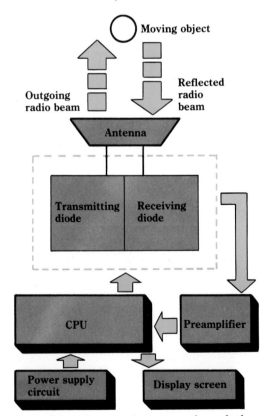

A diode sends out microwaves through the antenna, which picks up reflected waves and feeds them to a second diode. The preamplifier boosts the signal; the CPU analyzes it and displays results on the screen.

Range of fire

Speed guns are able to clock objects traveling between 0 and 199 miles per hour, up to a distance of about 200 feet.

Readings are taken about once per second anywhere within the conical field of the beam, as shown below.

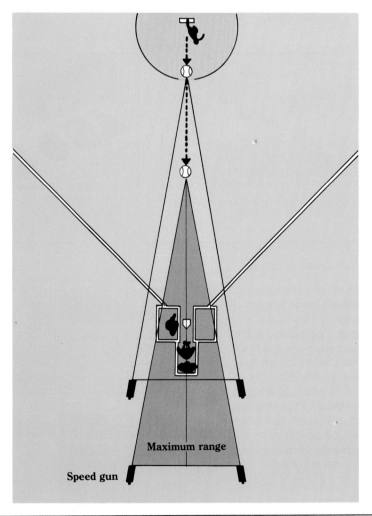

How Is Modern Printing Done?

Professional printing houses use three main methods for transferring letters and images onto the page. These are relief printing, intaglio, and lithography, each of which has a different way of preparing the plate that delivers the ink. The relief technique—little changed from the 1400s, when Johannes Gutenberg invented modern printing—involves carving a plate either mechanically or with chemicals to create raised surfaces that carry ink. Intaglio, or gravure, printing reverses that process, etching into a plate all the areas that are to be printed. Lithography, the most common type of printing used today, employs a plate that is specially treated so that ink sticks to some areas and is repelled from others.

In the type of lithography called offset, the plate is pressed against a sheet of rubber, called a blanket, mounted on a turning drum. Paper in cut sheets or a continuous sheet called a web feeds under tension past this drum and receives the quick-drying ink. This method yields sharp, high-quality letters and images and is generally considered the best all-around method, although relief printing produces clearer letters and intaglio richer color tones and shadings.

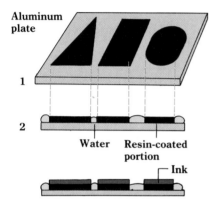

Aluminum plate

1

2

Water   Resin-coated portion

Ink

The offset method

A photosensitive aluminum plate (1) is sandwiched with a film negative of a page to be printed. The plate is then exposed to light and rinsed, bearing coated areas that repel water but accept ink (2). Mounted on a cylinder, an offset plate passes its ink to a rubber blanket (3), which transfers the ink onto the taut paper, called a web (4).

Plate drum

Rubber blanket drum

3

Rubber blanket drum

Paper

Pressure drum

4

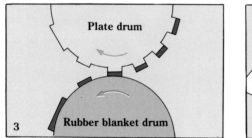
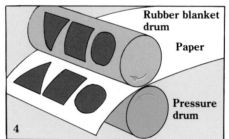

Four-color printing

To achieve lifelike color, printers break images down into four basic hues: cyan (blue), yellow, magenta (red), and black. The four colors are applied as tiny dots, the size of which determines the detail of the resulting print. Printers carefully balance the colors to produce realistic images like the one at far right.

Cyan plate

Yellow plate

Magenta plate

Black plate

Sheet-fed two-color offset

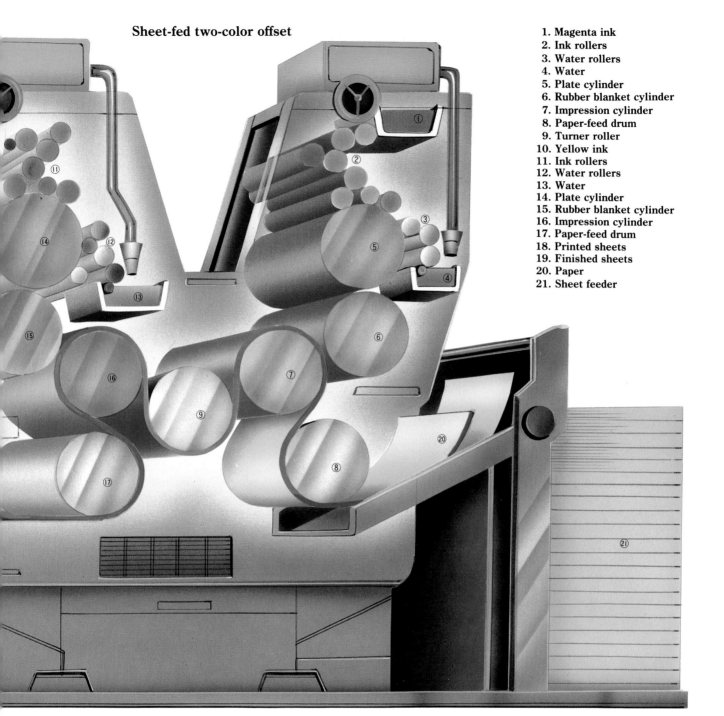

1. Magenta ink
2. Ink rollers
3. Water rollers
4. Water
5. Plate cylinder
6. Rubber blanket cylinder
7. Impression cylinder
8. Paper-feed drum
9. Turner roller
10. Yellow ink
11. Ink rollers
12. Water rollers
13. Water
14. Plate cylinder
15. Rubber blanket cylinder
16. Impression cylinder
17. Paper-feed drum
18. Printed sheets
19. Finished sheets
20. Paper
21. Sheet feeder

A single pass through this high-speed press yields a two-color print. For four colors, printers must change inks and reprint.

Relief printing

The forerunner of modern printing techniques, the relief method uses raised areas to carry ink. Preparing this type of plate requires more labor and is more costly than either intaglio or offset printing.

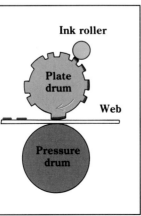

Intaglio printing

The ink-carrying portions of an intaglio, or gravure, plate are etched into its surface. As the drum turns, a knife, called the doctor blade, scrapes excess ink off the plate's surface. Ink left in the recesses is then transferred under high pressure onto the web.

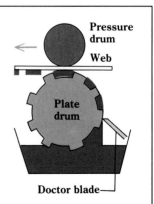

How Do Metal Detectors Operate?

Airport security gates, treasure sweepers for hunting lost change or jewelry on the beach, traffic switches, and coin slots in vending machines have one thing in common. They all exploit the fact that a piece of metal passing through a magnetic force field has one or more of its physical properties changed in a way that can be picked up by a sensor. Each type of metal detector contains a transmission element for generating a magnetic field and a receiving element for translating a secondary physical change into an electronic signal that registers on a dial or triggers a sonic alarm.

The simplest of these devices generates an electrical current that runs through a coil of wire, producing a magnetic field. When the coil passes over a piece of metal, the metal induces a second magnetic field which interferes with the first one and reverses the flow of electricity in the coil. This reversal is picked up by electronic circuitry. More sophisticated detectors that screen for concealed weapons, bombs, or bits of metal contaminating food, paper pulp, or raw plastic may contain additional coils and computer chips that boost their sensitivity.

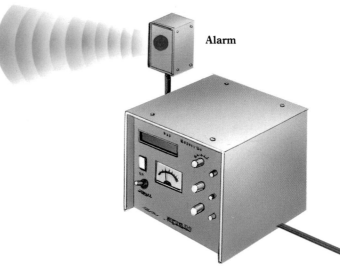

Alarm

Control box

To make sure that a security alarm sounds only if there is an unusual amount of metal, guards adjust the sensitivity on a control box like the one shown above.

A passenger prepares to enter an airport security gate.

Measuring magnetic fields

When a metallic object passes through a security gate *(below)*, the flux, or strength and extent of the magnetic field, increases. The rise in flux is accompanied by a voltage increase in the current flowing through the receiver coils, which triggers an alarm.

Two magnetic responses

Nickel, iron, and other easily magnetized metals enhance a magnetic field *(below)*, while copper, aluminum, and other less easily magnetized ones do not *(bottom)*.

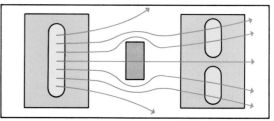

Nickel or iron attracts magnetic lines of force.

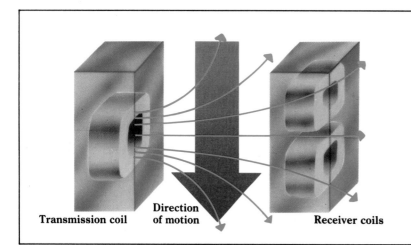

Transmission coil   Direction of motion   Receiver coils

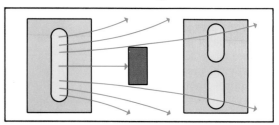

Copper repels the magnetic field.

Security checkpoint

To ferret out hidden guns or other weapons, airports and office buildings rely on security gates like the one at right. A series of coils scan a person's body and alert guards when sizable amounts of metal—possibly caused by the presence of weapons—are detected.

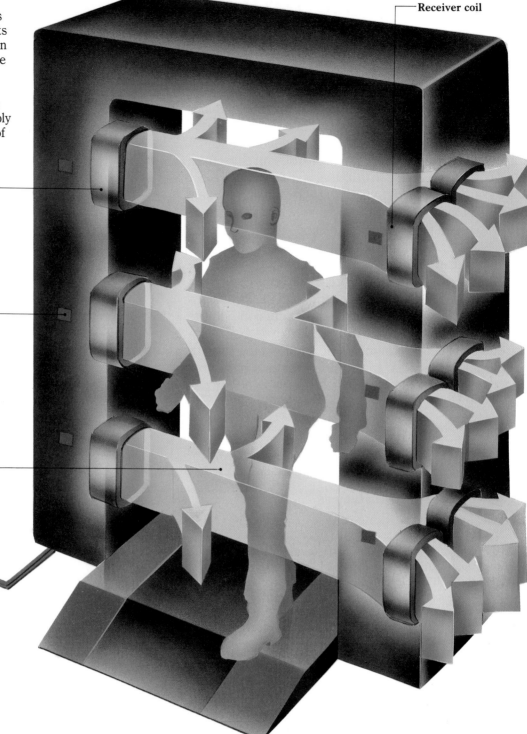

Receiver coil

Transmission coil

Detector lamp

Lines of magnetic force

Detecting ferromagnetic metals

The ferromagnetic materials nickel, iron, and cobalt become easily magnetized when exposed to a magnetic field. The special metal detector at left locates buried metals of this sort. The magnetic fields in its two coils cancel each other out until exposed to a metal object. Then, the object's induced magnetism trips an electrical gate, sending a low current from the receiver coil to the detector's electronic circuitry.

What Is a Vacuum Pump?

Modern science and technology have many needs for vacuums, which are vital to the proper performance of numerous instruments and experiments. To create vacuums, technicians remove virtually all matter within a closed space such as a tube or chamber. Vacuum pumps are ingenious devices for voiding gases, generally air, by mechanical or chemical means. Oil-pressure vacuum pumps compress gases with a twirling rotor and eject them through an exhaust valve. Vapor-diffusion models carry out the same task without moving parts. In them, jets of vaporized fluids force atoms and molecules of gas down a baffled chamber, reducing its pressure.

Vacuums are frequently measured in terms of the torr, a unit representing the pressure on a column of mercury. Low-level vacuums rank about 25 torr; high-level ones, which can be produced by diffusion pumps, rank from .001 to .000001 torr. Producing higher vacuums requires specialty pumps that employ electrons to drive out gas molecules. In the lab, scientists have created vacuums equal to one-billionth of a billionth the pressure of Earth's atmosphere at sea level.

A turbomolecular pump

A machine that creates vacuums

A powerful motor turns interlocking blades inside the casing of a turbomolecular pump *(below),* which produces high-level vacuums. Gas molecules are shunted against the walls and pushed downward, causing them to exit through the air exhaust.

Movable blade

Stationary blade

Air intake

Air exhaust

Motor

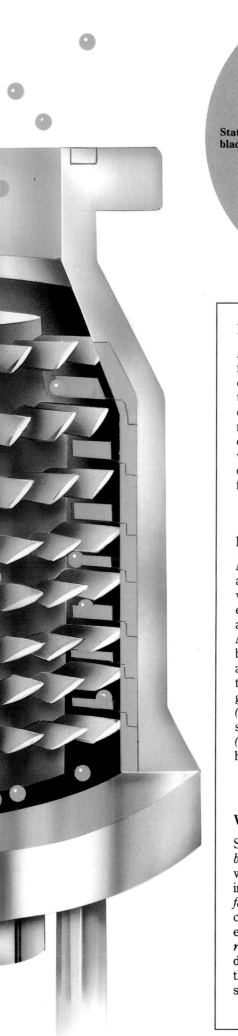

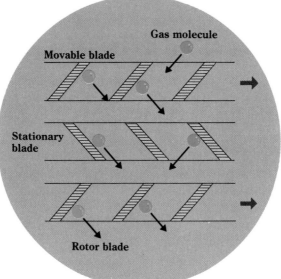

Gas molecule

Movable blade

Stationary blade

Rotor blade

Playing molecular pinball

A series of blades, some fixed, some spinning on a central shaft, serve to guide molecules inside a turbomolecular pump. Because of the angle of the blades, molecules can only ricochet downward toward the exhaust port.

Diffusion pump

A heater at the bottom of this diffusion pump vaporizes oil or mercury, which rises and is sprayed through jet nozzles against the chamber walls. The spray forces molecules and atoms of gas out the exhaust valve. After hitting the water-cooled walls, the vapor condenses and returns to the boiler for reheating and recirculation.

Rotary oil-seal pump

An oil-seal pump moves gas out of an airtight chamber and expels it with a rotary plunger. Gas at higher pressure moves into the pump and is pushed ahead of the rotor. As the rotor moves toward the bottom of its cycle, a sliding blade attached to it drops down, dividing the chamber in two and barring the gas's continued forward motion *(near right)*. The rotor's finishing stroke compresses the trapped gas *(dark blue)*, forcing it out of an exhaust valve *(far right)*.

Water-seal pump

Spinning blades force water *(light blue)* against the chamber wall of a water-seal pump. Gases from the inlet trapped in the impeller *(top, far right)* are compressed in the central portion of the pump and ejected through an outlet *(top, near right)*. Water-seal pumps can produce only low-level vacuums, so they are rarely used, but they are simple to run and maintain.

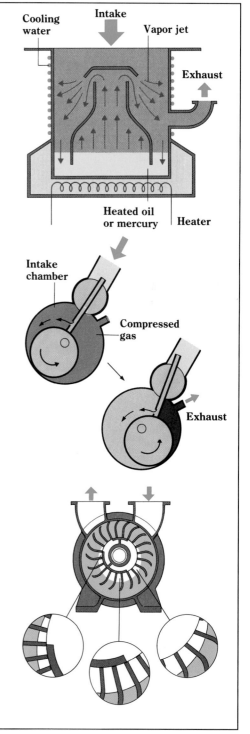

Cooling water

Intake

Vapor jet

Exhaust

Heated oil or mercury | Heater

Intake chamber

Compressed gas

Exhaust

How Is the Flow of Fluids Measured?

During many industrial processes, technicians must monitor the rate at which liquids, gases, and vapors of various sorts stream through pipes or machinery. Also, gas and water companies must keep track of how much of their product customers use. There are dozens of instruments for measuring the flow of fluids, gauging either volume or velocity. Some of these devices work by blocking the normal flow of the fluid and then determining the change in pressure that results as the fluid detours around the barrier. Others use rotating blades whose rate of spin depends on the strength of the fluid's flow. Still others sense a fluid's electrical conductivity or bombard it with ultrasonic waves to gain readings on the volume that has passed in a given period.

Connecting tube

Connecting tube

Differential pressure sensor

The sensor at left and below translates a difference in pressure between streams of a flowing liquid into an electrical signal that registers on a gauge. Vibrating diaphragms trigger a change in the ability of capacitor plates to hold a charge and cause an electrical current proportional to the liquid's flow to register.

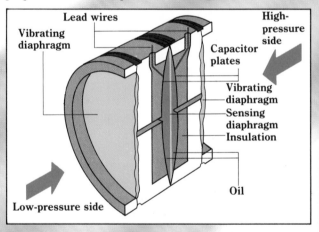

Lead wires

High-pressure side

Vibrating diaphragm

Capacitor plates

Vibrating diaphragm

Sensing diaphragm

Insulation

Oil

Low-pressure side

Differential pressure sensor

Differential signal generator

Differential flow device

The orifice plate, shown inside a water pipe *(below, left),* restricts the water flow, causing it to accelerate as it passes through the opening. The difference in speed is detected by the differential pressure sensor.

Aperture

Measuring other fluids

Measuring the flow rate of thicker fluids such as oil requires meters different from the one shown at left. Hourglass-shaped venturi tubes, protruding flow nozzles, and orifice plates having holes in other shapes and locations are used for such substances, as shown below.

A venturi tube and pressure

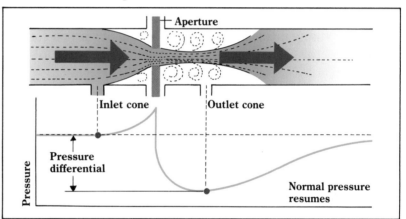

Aperture

Inlet cone   Outlet cone

Pressure differential

Normal pressure resumes

Pressure

When a fluid enters a venturi tube, the fluid's pressure drops *(above),* an effect described in 1738 by mathematician Daniel Bernoulli. Knowing the magnitude of that drop, technicians can calculate flow rate using a formula Bernoulli derived.

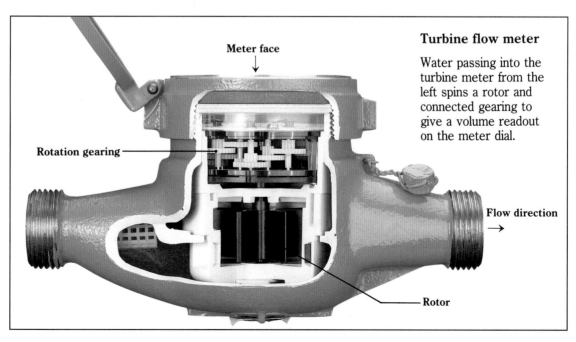

Meter face

Rotation gearing

Turbine flow meter

Water passing into the turbine meter from the left spins a rotor and connected gearing to give a volume readout on the meter dial.

Flow direction

Rotor

How Are Precision Measurements Made?

In the everyday world, a common ruler is all that is needed to measure the length of things. In factories and scientific laboratories, however, it is sometimes necessary to know the size of objects within exceedingly small tolerances or to take the dimensions of extremely thin wires, sheets, or solid bodies. For these purposes, instruments called micrometers and vernier calipers, or slide calipers, are used.

Micrometers use two scales consisting of graduations on a spindle and a thimble that take readings down to within thousandths of an inch, depending on the pitch of the screw threads on the spindle and the number of divisions on the thimble scale. Vernier calipers operate on a similar principle but pair two linear scales on a mechanism that allows them to slide past each other. The divisions of the auxiliary, or vernier, scale are usually .9 times those of the main scale, and readings are taken by setting the vernier scale's zero to the observed measurement of a specimen. Then, an additional decimal place of accuracy can be gained by noting where the graduations on the two scales line up again and reading the number off the vernier scale. Both instruments are invaluable in manufacturing machine parts and sheeting of various sorts, and in numerous other scientific and engineering enterprises.

A micrometer

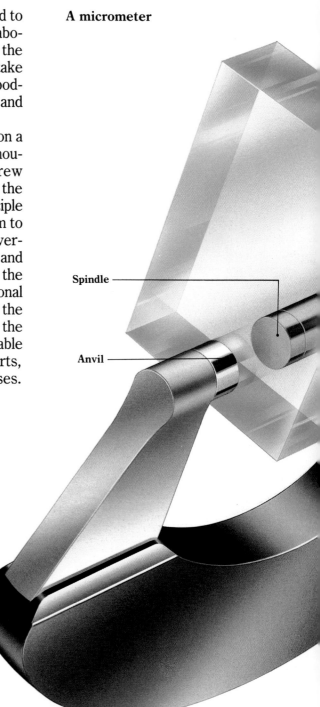

Spindle

Anvil

Basis of a meter's accuracy

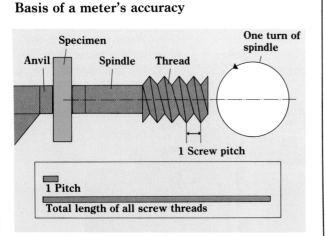

Specimen

Anvil   Spindle   Thread

One turn of spindle

1 Screw pitch

1 Pitch

Total length of all screw threads

With each full turn, the micrometer's screw advances the length of one screw pitch.

A micrometer grips a specimen between an anvil and a spindle that is mounted on a stable, U-shaped frame. The spindle's threading has been carefully machined to a high degree of evenness. The turning spindle advances through a nut with matching threading inside the thimble. The motion registers on two scales, one on the spindle and one on the thimble. A ratchet at the far end stops the spindle when pressure reaches a certain level, indicating the proper measurement.

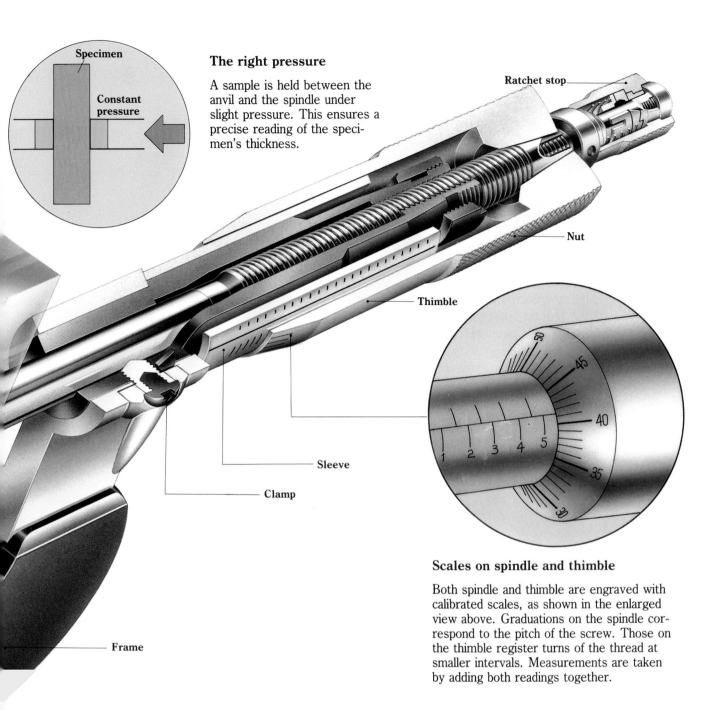

The right pressure

A sample is held between the anvil and the spindle under slight pressure. This ensures a precise reading of the specimen's thickness.

Specimen

Constant pressure

Ratchet stop

Nut

Thimble

Sleeve

Clamp

Frame

Scales on spindle and thimble

Both spindle and thimble are engraved with calibrated scales, as shown in the enlarged view above. Graduations on the spindle correspond to the pitch of the screw. Those on the thimble register turns of the thread at smaller intervals. Measurements are taken by adding both readings together.

Slide calipers

The movable jaw of a vernier caliper slides along a calibrated scale *(below, left)*. The calipers can take width readings *(center)* or interior dimension readings *(below, right)*. Readings from two scales, the main one on the caliper body and an auxiliary on the jaw, are added together to obtain measurements.

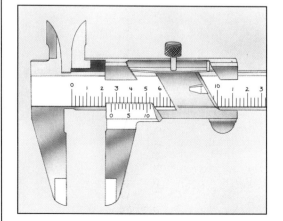

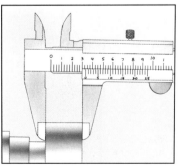

Measuring an outside dimension

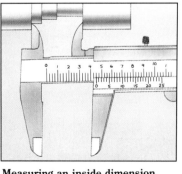

Measuring an inside dimension

How Can Air Be Purified?

The windows of modern buildings are often sealed shut to improve energy efficiency. To keep the air inside breathable, heating and cooling systems must provide fresh air that is vented into the buildings. In addition, circulating air has to be cycled through special filtering systems to remove smoke and dust particles, as well as pollen and microorganisms capable of triggering allergies or transmitting disease.

Commonly, these systems employ a series of ever-finer filters that trap pollutants of smaller and smaller size. Other elements, including fans and dehumidifiers, make up an air circulation system, which in some buildings is regulated from a central control room.

Step-by-step cleaning of air

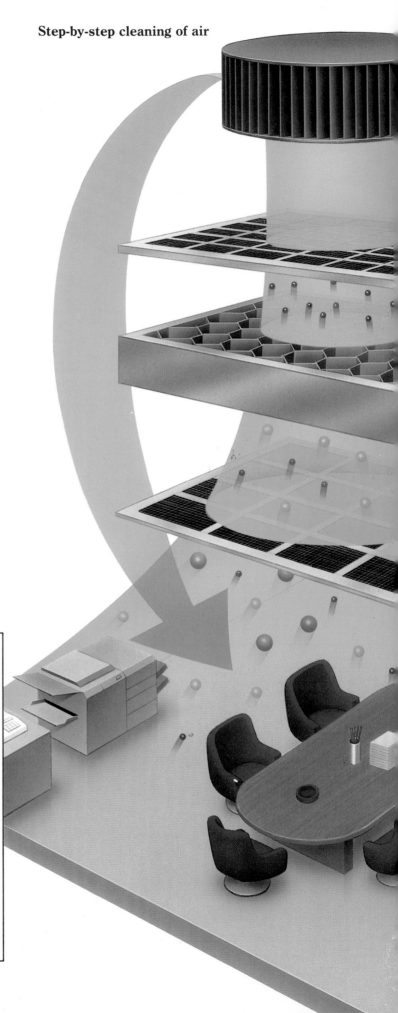

Dirty air is drawn up through a series of filters by a fan, which re-circulates air after it has been cleaned.

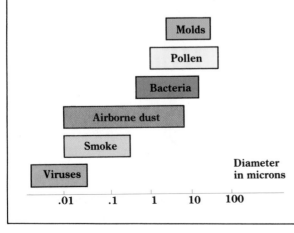

Dirt and dust by diameter

Pollutants floating in air range from mold spores to viruses visible only under electron microscopes. A micron is 100 millionths of a centimeter, or 39.4 millionths of an inch.

Molds	
Pollen	
Bacteria	
Airborne dust	
Smoke	
Viruses	

Diameter in microns

.01 .1 1 10 100

An electrical trap

Particles entering an electrostatic filter gain a positive charge and as a result stick to the negatively charged walls *(left and below, right)*.

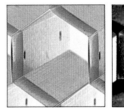

Filter before use

Filter after use

An activated carbon filter removes the tiniest particles, especially those that cause odors.

An electrostatic filter snares small charged particles by electrical means.

A mesh prefilter of spun metal, fiberglass, or plastic catches large particles.

Purifying an entire building

A basement air-conditioning system can provide heating, cooling, humidity control, and filtering for an entire building, recirculating air through a series of vents and ducts.

Clean air

Dirty air

Air-conditioning system

Supply duct

Exhaust duct

What Is a Self-Raising Crane?

Swivel platform

The construction of skyscrapers requires a special breed of crane that is able to jack itself higher as floors are added. The self-raising crane does just that by extending the climbing frame, which is a kind of hydraulic scaffold. As the frame goes up unit by unit, the crane itself hoists sections resembling reinforced steel cages from the ground and slips them into place using the climbing frame as a guide. The sections are then bolted to the top of the towerlike mast. Once the top floor of the building is completed, the crane has to be dismantled and is brought down to the ground in small sections, in a time-consuming process that may take several weeks.

Upper climbing frame

Mast

Hydraulic cylinder

Lower climbing frame

Dismantling a crane

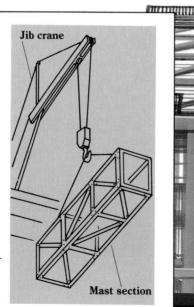

Jib crane

When a building is completed, the climbing crane is taken apart piece by piece. First, the crane operator raises a smaller crane, called a jib, onto the roof. Using this crane, workers unhook the upper sections of the climbing crane and lower them to the ground. Mast sections are similarly removed and lowered. Finally, the jib itself is disassembled and ferried to the ground in pieces on the construction elevator.

Mast section

Main jib

Operator's cab

Parts of a crane

A cab and platform sit atop the hydraulic lift and uppermost mast section. Attached to the movable platform is a boom—the main jib—which has a winch and pulley at its tip.

An elevating process

The source of a climbing crane's strength lies in its powerful hydraulic cylinder, which notches the climbing frame upward by turns, as shown below. The force of the boom's interlocking cylinders propels the cab and platform upward along the sectioned mast, carrying the mast along with them.

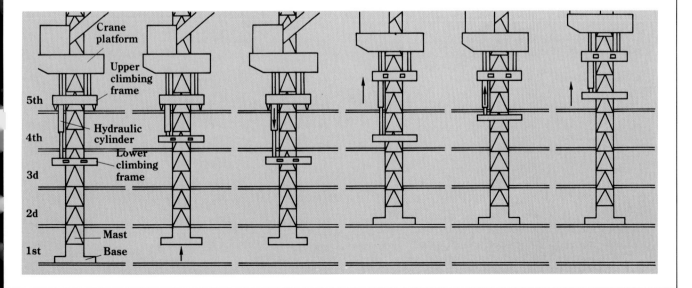

Crane platform

Upper climbing frame

5th

Hydraulic cylinder

4th

Lower climbing frame

3d

2d

Mast

1st   Base

3

An Explosion in Office Equipment

As recently as the 1960s, the mainstays of offices were electric typewriters and telephones. Few businesses could afford bulky and balking computers, which in those days took up whole rooms. But the development of ever-smaller microchips, or integrated circuits, during the last three decades has prompted an explosion in office equipment. Be it desktop personal computer, fax machine, or color photocopier, all are benefiting from the microchip's unparalleled ability to process data. Integrated circuits have improved the efficiency of other machines long in use in office buildings, including elevators and vending machines.

In the future, however, still-tinier computers may make office buildings obsolete. Workers equipped with notebook-size computers that serve as phones, pagers, faxes, and datalinks to virtually any other computer in the world may report only rarely to a central office, and conduct almost all their business at home or on the road. This chapter looks at the new office machines and how they make life easier in the workplace.

Machines found in the modern office include, clockwise from top left, escalators, IC cards, phones, elevators, fax machines, vending machines, color photocopiers, and fire alarms.

How Do Telephones Transmit Voices?

Alexander Graham Bell's 1876 patent on the telephone specified a simple system made up of a metal reed, an electric coil, and a vibrating diaphragm. Modern phones still use diaphragms to turn voices into electrical signals that are transmitted over phone lines. But today microchip technology converts and amplifies incoming signals into clear and distinct speech. Modern phones convey not only voices but also text and images, and they provide linkups between far-flung computers.

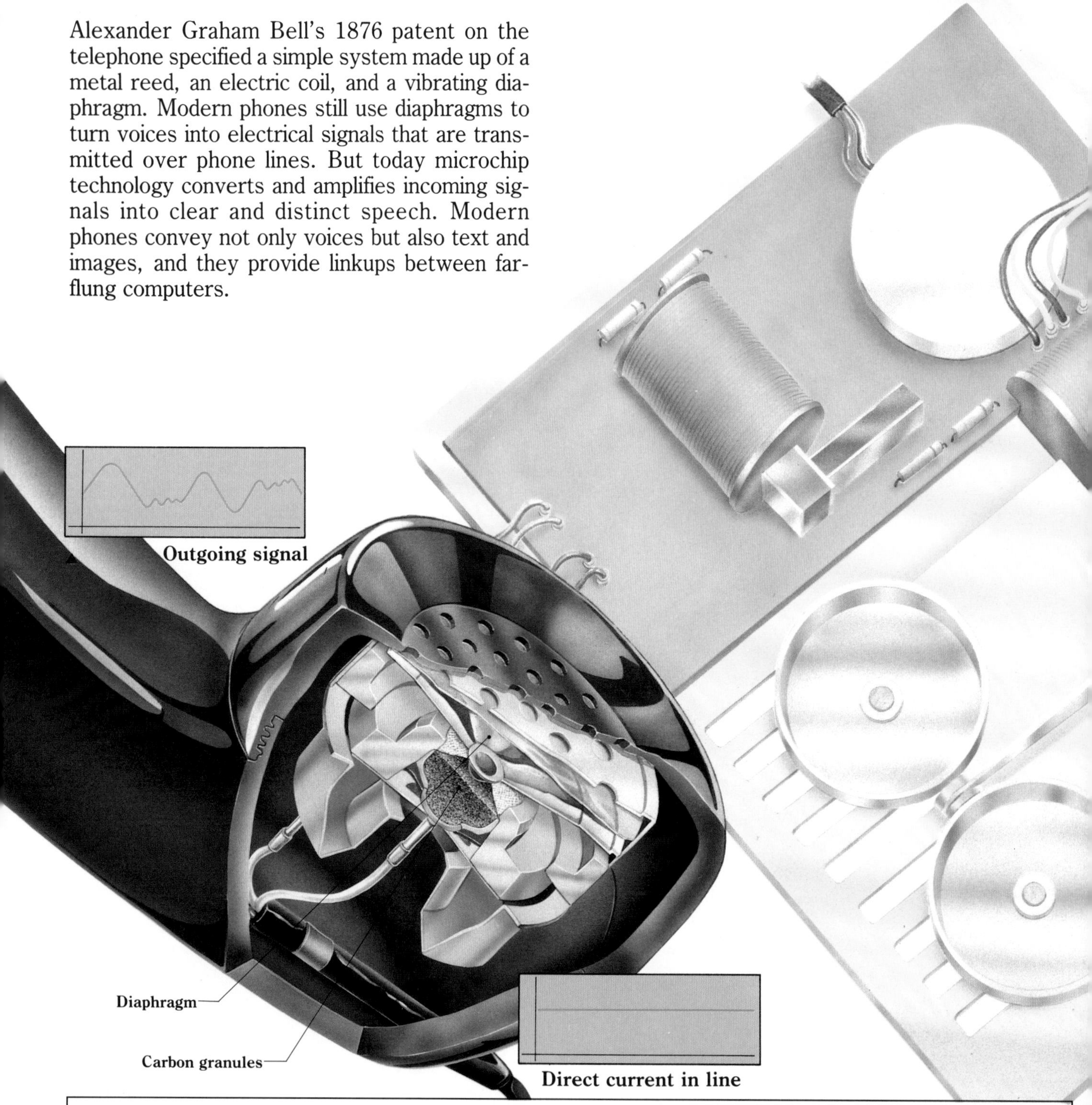

Outgoing signal

Diaphragm

Carbon granules

Direct current in line

Filtering voices through carbon

Electrically conductive carbon granules in the mouthpiece are sensitive to vibrations induced in the diaphragm by a voice. Even a slight motion of the diaphragm causes the tightly packed granules to shift, yielding a variable flow of current that constitutes the sound waves that make up the voice. A microchip in the phone boosts this signal for transmission over phone lines.

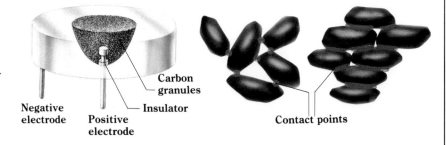

Negative electrode

Positive electrode

Carbon granules

Insulator

Contact points

Cutaway view of a handset

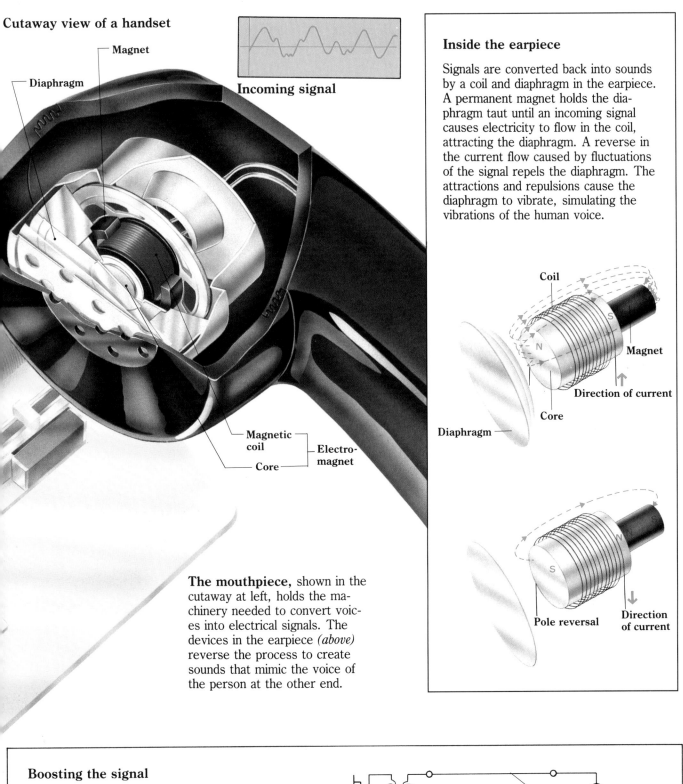

Diaphragm

Magnet

Incoming signal

Magnetic coil

Core } **Electro-magnet**

The mouthpiece, shown in the cutaway at left, holds the machinery needed to convert voices into electrical signals. The devices in the earpiece *(above)* reverse the process to create sounds that mimic the voice of the person at the other end.

Inside the earpiece

Signals are converted back into sounds by a coil and diaphragm in the earpiece. A permanent magnet holds the diaphragm taut until an incoming signal causes electricity to flow in the coil, attracting the diaphragm. A reverse in the current flow caused by fluctuations of the signal repels the diaphragm. The attractions and repulsions cause the diaphragm to vibrate, simulating the vibrations of the human voice.

Coil

N

S

Magnet

Direction of current

Core

Diaphragm

S

Pole reversal

Direction of current

Boosting the signal

An electrical signal coming from a phone *(blue)* decreases with distance, so phone companies boost the current at exchange offices before passing it through switching circuitry *(diagramed at right)* that sends it on to the target phone *(pink)*.

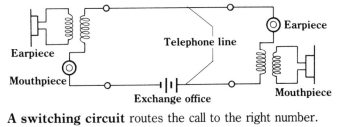

Earpiece

Mouthpiece

Telephone line

Earpiece

Mouthpiece

Exchange office

A switching circuit routes the call to the right number.

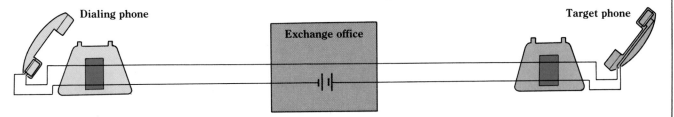

Dialing phone

Exchange office

Target phone

What Is inside a Vending Machine?

Although simple on the outside, vending machines have a complex array of mechanisms inside. These devices assess the value of coins and eject those that are counterfeit or wrong; they regulate temperatures of heating and cooling units, and they drop the products into the vending slot.

In some machines coin testers function mechanically, by routing coins past a series of levers that open only if the coins are the right size and weight. Coins are otherwise diverted through swinging gates into the return chute. In state-of-the-art machines this same job is done by electric sensors, which test metal content; magnets, which check on size; and light-emitting devices, which monitor speed and diameter.

To control temperatures for hot or cold drinks and food, modern vending machines are armed with thermostats and microprocessors. Although snack foods and drinks are still the main items supplied by vending machines, the machines have become so versatile that a customer can buy all the components of a meal from them.

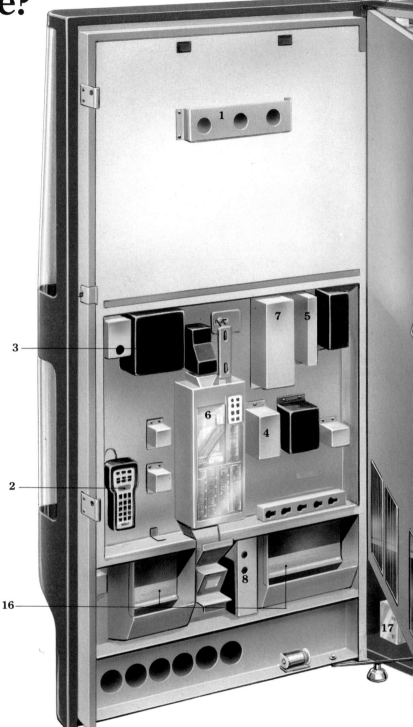

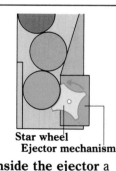

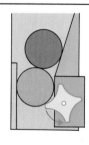

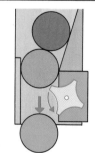

Cans, one at a time

A device called a star wheel rations out cans, so only one falls for each payment. Set at the bottom of the product racks, star wheels vary in shape according to the products they dole out. This four-sided model rotates a quarter turn at a time, letting a single can slip into the delivery chute.

Star wheel
Ejector mechanism

Inside the ejector a star wheel holds a can tightly in place.

The star wheel responds to the control box with a quarter turn.

The next can in the rack slips down and is caught by the wheel.

Inside the machine

9

10

12

11

13

14

15

Keeping out counterfeits

From the vendor's point of view, the coin sorter is the most important part of a vending machine. To function properly, the machine must sort coins, spot fake ones, retain only good ones, and return correct change in addition to delivering the product. Some machines also accept paper currency, which is optically scanned for authenticity and face value.

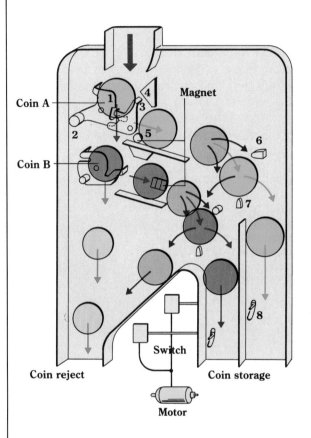

Coin A

Magnet

Coin B

Coin reject

Switch

Coin storage

Motor

Coins fed into a vending machine (1) take indirect paths to the coin holder, as shown above with two coins, A *(blue)* and B *(pink)*. Coin A drops into a pivoting cradle (3) and, if heavier than the counterbalance (2), rolls forward, down a rail. Larger coins are caught by a stop (4). If coin A is of the proper metal composition, a magnet (5) alters the coin's speed just enough so that it will fall into the coin storage (8) rather than bounce off stops (6 and 7), as do the purple and green coins, which then move into the coin-reject chute. Coin B, which is smaller than coin A, is sorted on a separate rail in the same manner.

How Can a Smart Card Store Data?

The integrated circuit (IC) logic card is known as the smart card because it can handle many functions. The card is marked with a magnetized strip, similar to those found on credit and automated bank teller cards, which contains a coded number assigned to it. The card also carries a tiny microchip that allows it to perform computations.

Able to hold about 100 times more information than simple magnetic cards, IC logic cards can be used to store a person's entire medical or banking record, in addition to the bearer's photograph, signature, and any other data that can be digitized and read by a scanner. Smart cards are still experimental, but they may one day replace magnetic cards altogether.

IC card, actual and magnified

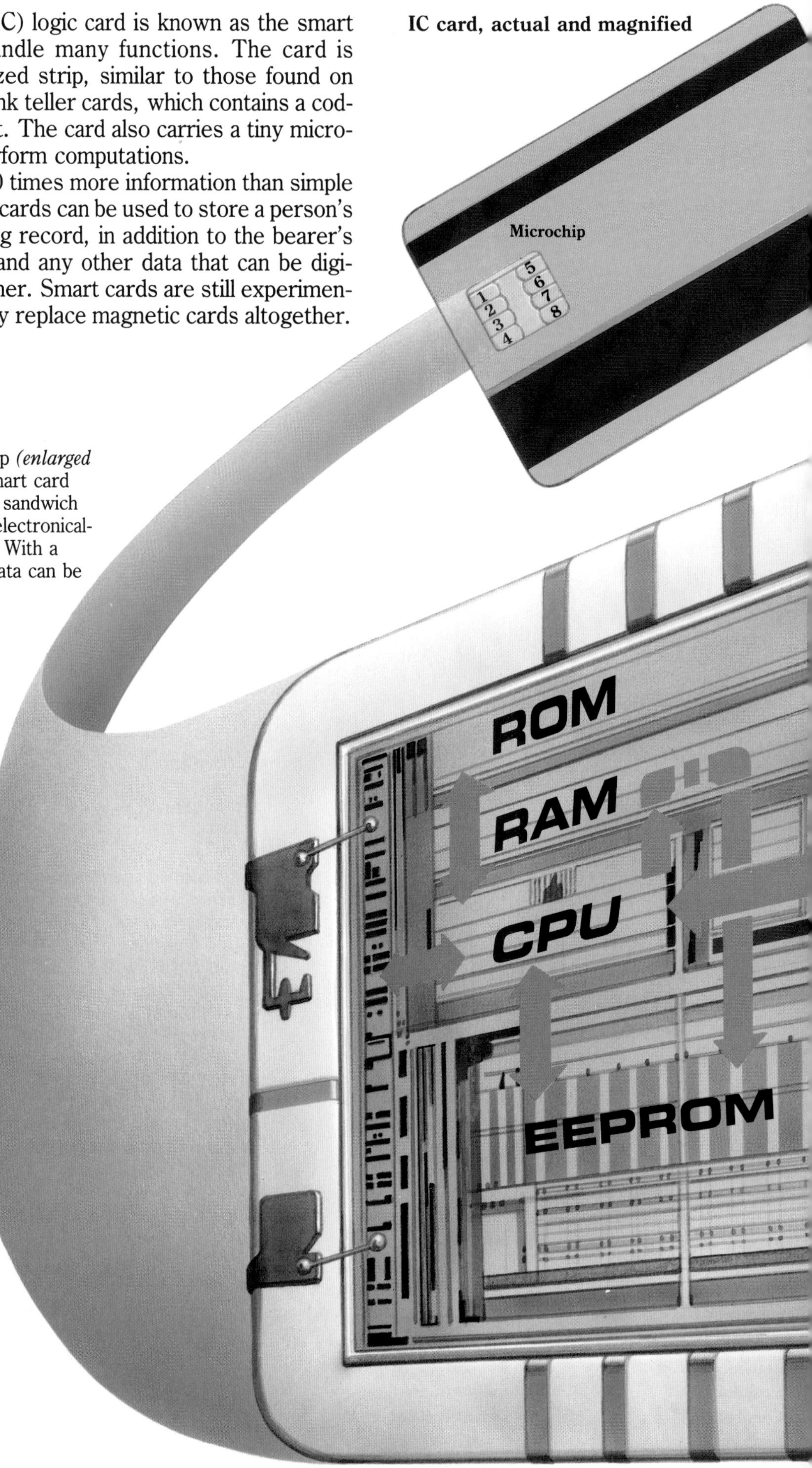

Microchip

The integrated circuit

An IC, also called a microchip *(enlarged at right),* is the heart of a smart card *(actual size top right).* A thin sandwich of silicon and metal, the IC electronically stores and retrieves data. With a smart card, some types of data can be altered, others cannot.

ROM

RAM

CPU

EEPROM

Inputs and outputs of the logic card's microchip	
1	Circuit voltage
2	Reset
3	Clock
4	Extra pin
5	Ground
6	Program supply voltage
7	Data input/output
8	Extra pin

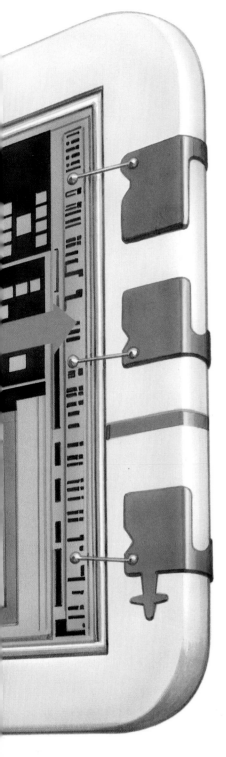

The function of external pins

The microchip on a smart card requires a series of external pins to connect it to a power supply and allow it to communicate with a terminal and other devices. The function of each pin on a typical IC card is listed at left.

Memory to prevent illegal entry

The smart card is equipped with three kinds of memory: The read-only memory (ROM) holds the card's operating system, which can be read but not altered by the user. The random-access memory (RAM) is a temporary storage point for computation—information that can be altered and is retained only as long as the card is plugged in. The electrically erasable, programmable read-only memory (EEPROM) can be altered only under special conditions. These programs make the smart card especially useful in restricting access to confidential information or sensitive areas—military installations, bank vaults, or other locations that must be secure. A password encoded in the secret zone of the card's programmable read-only memory will enable the cardholder to gain access to special places. For an even safer method of establishing the identity of a cardholder, a computerized record of a physical trait, such as an eye print or a thumbprint of the bearer, can be stored in the card. This information is verified at the entrance by a scanner that will let only that one person pass.

How Do Copiers Reproduce Colors?

To copy a document, a black-and-white photocopier first flashes a light onto the paper. The light reflects only off the white parts of the original. This reflection goes through a lens onto a turning metal drum. The drum has a negative electrical charge but loses that charge in areas struck by the light. As the drum continues turning past a toning station, positively charged black toner particles bind to the negatively charged areas. The particles are transferred to a sheet of paper, which passes through a heated roller that permanently bonds the toner, yielding a copy.

Color copiers employ a similar process, using cyan (blue), magenta (red), and yellow filters. The reflected light is amplified with a charge-coupled device (CCD), which directs a laser beam. Separate stations apply cyan, magenta, yellow, and black toner, to create a color image.

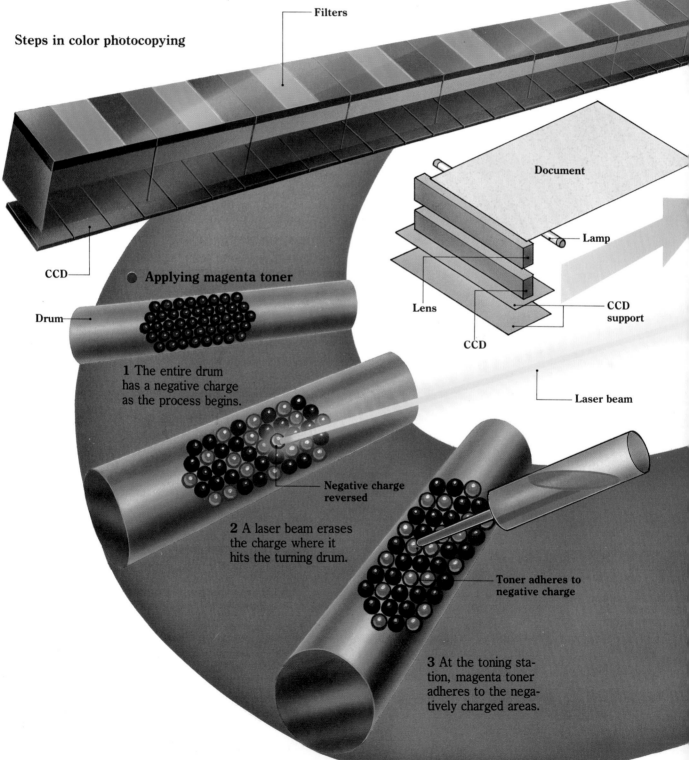

Steps in color photocopying

Filters

CCD

Drum

● **Applying magenta toner**

1 The entire drum has a negative charge as the process begins.

Negative charge reversed

2 A laser beam erases the charge where it hits the turning drum.

Document

Lamp

Lens

CCD support

CCD

Laser beam

Toner adheres to negative charge

3 At the toning station, magenta toner adheres to the negatively charged areas.

— Document

Filtering light to make color

Lying under the glass are a lens and a ribbon of three color filters. Beneath the filters, a CCD sensor picks up light signals and amplifies them.

— Lens

— Filters

Light source

The filters and CCD are long and narrow, allowing the photocopier to scan documents as a series of smaller units, called pixels.

Heat roller —

— CCD

The CCD amplifies faint light that strikes it. Here, a CCD directs the action of a laser beam *(above)*.

Laser

Fixing an image

A hot roller applies finishing touches, fusing the three toners to the page.

Black for sharpness

As a last step, black toner is applied to areas where all three colors have already been laid down. This creates realistically shaded images.

4 The magenta toner from the drum sticks to the paper, which in turn receives layers of cyan, yellow, and black toner.

Cyan and yellow pixels are applied over the magenta as the paper passes by two more stations.

Photocopier profiled

The cutaway at right shows the key elements of a color photocopier, including paper trays sticking out of the sides.

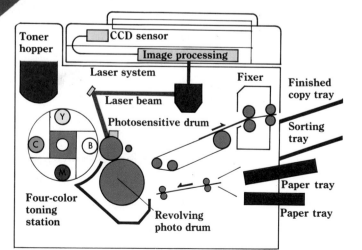

Toner hopper

CCD sensor

Image processing

Laser system

Laser beam

Fixer

Finished copy tray

Photosensitive drum

Sorting tray

Y

C   B

M

Four-color toning station

Revolving photo drum

Paper tray

Paper tray

Are All Fire Alarm Systems the Same?

Special sensors in automatic fire alarms detect smoke or heat, and sometimes both, before a fire spreads. Photoelectric sensors react to the presence of tiny particles of smoke. Heat and rate-of-rise sensors respond, in turn, when temperatures top set limits, usually 135° F. inside a home, and when they soar upward a given number of degrees within a certain time, usually 15° F. per minute. Each type of sensor then triggers the sounding of an alarm, which, like the sensor, is powered by a battery. Because these devices are extremely sensitive, they can signal that fire has broken out before people would notice it or warn them while they are asleep in their homes.

Alarm installation

When wiring a multistory building, installers place heat and smoke detectors on each floor, as shown in this diagram of a three-story structure. A control unit locates the source of any alarm.

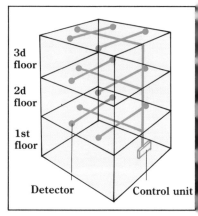

A variety of fire alarms

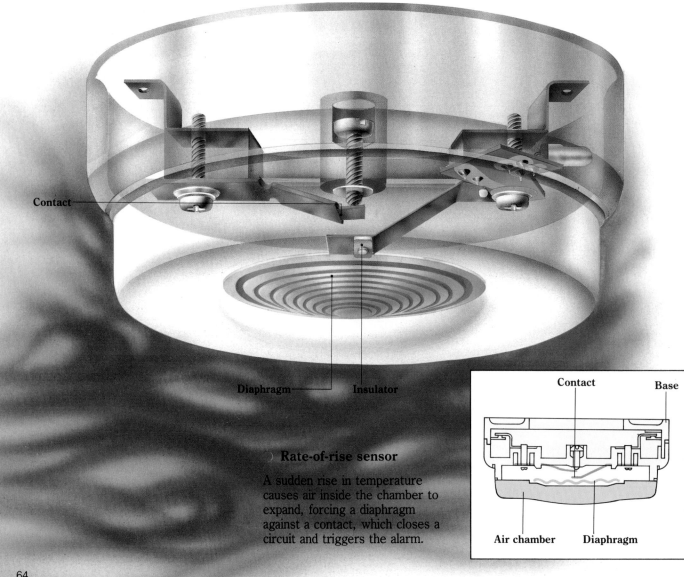

Contact

Diaphragm — Insulator

Rate-of-rise sensor

A sudden rise in temperature causes air inside the chamber to expand, forcing a diaphragm against a contact, which closes a circuit and triggers the alarm.

Contact   Base

Air chamber   Diaphragm

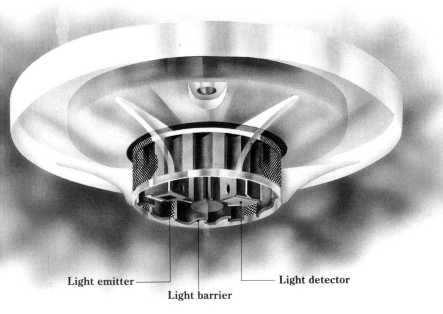

Photoelectric sensor

Smoke particles entering the chamber interrupt a steady beam of light, causing less light to register at a detector and triggering the sounding of the alarm.

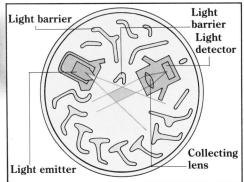

Light emitter — Light detector

Light barrier

Light barrier
Light barrier
Light detector
Light emitter
Collecting lens

Standard heat sensor

Bimetal sensors use two kinds of metal that expand at different rates when exposed to heat. If the sensor expands sufficiently, it causes a contact spring to close a circuit that sets off the alarm.

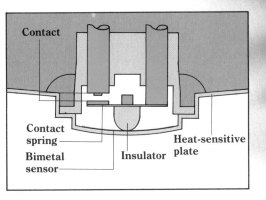

Contact

Contact spring
Bimetal sensor
Insulator
Heat-sensitive plate

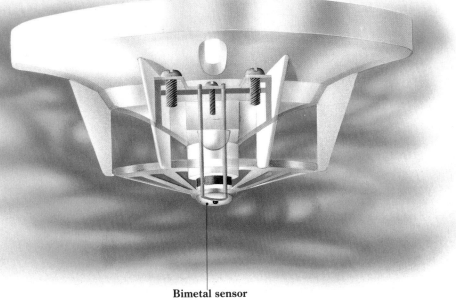

Bimetal sensor

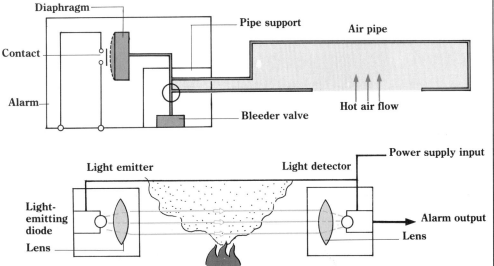

Pneumatic tube detector

This type of detector consists of a tubing circuit filled with air. When heat reaches the tubing, it causes the air inside to expand, forcing the diaphragm outward to close a circuit and sound the alarm.

Diaphragm
Contact
Alarm
Pipe support
Air pipe
Hot air flow
Bleeder valve

Separated photoelectrics

Light from an emitter is aimed at a detector on the far wall. Smoke blocks the beams, and the detector signals an alert.

Light emitter
Light detector
Power supply input
Light-emitting diode
Lens
Alarm output
Lens

How Do Elevators and Escalators Run?

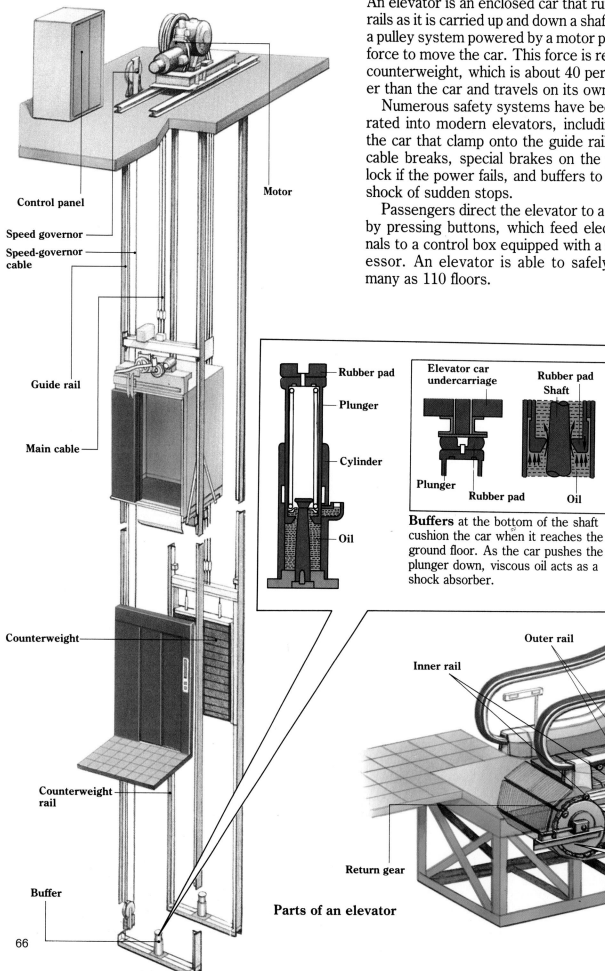

An elevator is an enclosed car that runs on guide rails as it is carried up and down a shaft. Typically a pulley system powered by a motor provides the force to move the car. This force is reduced by a counterweight, which is about 40 percent heavier than the car and travels on its own rails.

Numerous safety systems have been incorporated into modern elevators, including jaws on the car that clamp onto the guide rails in case a cable breaks, special brakes on the pulley that lock if the power fails, and buffers to reduce the shock of sudden stops.

Passengers direct the elevator to a given floor by pressing buttons, which feed electronic signals to a control box equipped with a microprocessor. An elevator is able to safely travel as many as 110 floors.

Control panel

Speed governor

Speed-governor cable

Guide rail

Main cable

Counterweight

Counterweight rail

Buffer

Motor

Rubber pad

Plunger

Cylinder

Oil

Elevator car undercarriage

Rubber pad
Shaft

Plunger

Rubber pad

Oil

Buffers at the bottom of the shaft cushion the car when it reaches the ground floor. As the car pushes the plunger down, viscous oil acts as a shock absorber.

Outer rail

Inner rail

Return gear

Parts of an elevator

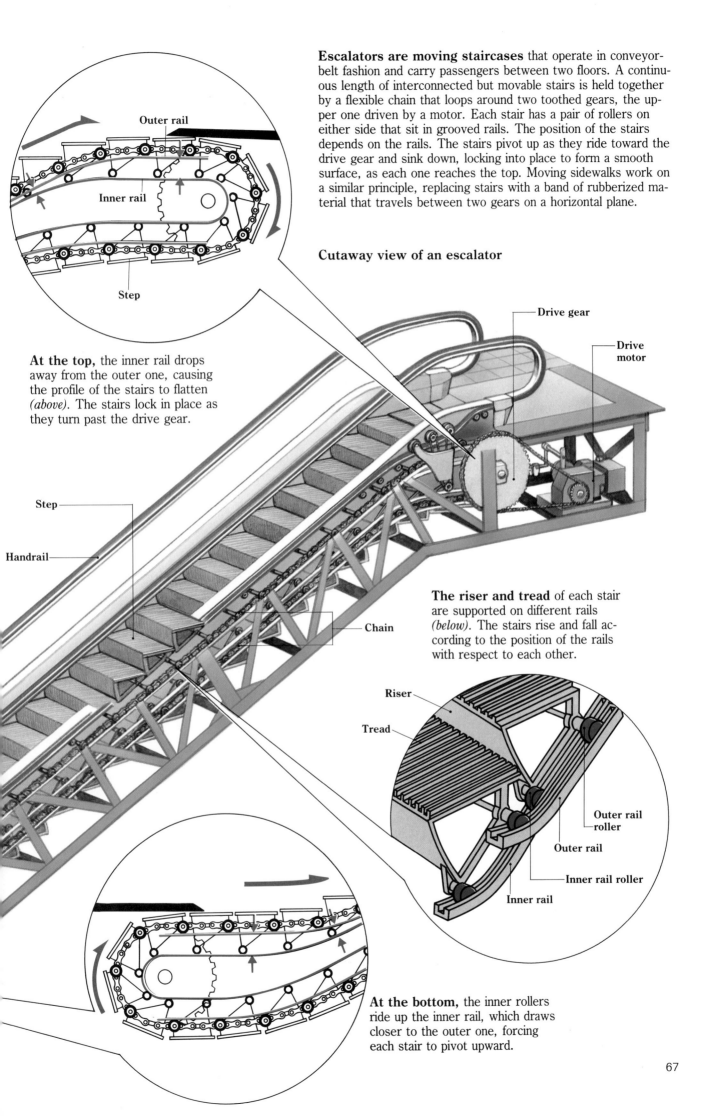

Outer rail

Inner rail

Step

Escalators are moving staircases that operate in conveyor-belt fashion and carry passengers between two floors. A continuous length of interconnected but movable stairs is held together by a flexible chain that loops around two toothed gears, the upper one driven by a motor. Each stair has a pair of rollers on either side that sit in grooved rails. The position of the stairs depends on the rails. The stairs pivot up as they ride toward the drive gear and sink down, locking into place to form a smooth surface, as each one reaches the top. Moving sidewalks work on a similar principle, replacing stairs with a band of rubberized material that travels between two gears on a horizontal plane.

Cutaway view of an escalator

— **Drive gear**

— **Drive motor**

At the top, the inner rail drops away from the outer one, causing the profile of the stairs to flatten *(above)*. The stairs lock in place as they turn past the drive gear.

Step —

Handrail—

— Chain

The riser and tread of each stair are supported on different rails *(below)*. The stairs rise and fall according to the position of the rails with respect to each other.

Riser —

Tread —

Outer rail roller

Outer rail

Inner rail roller

Inner rail

At the bottom, the inner rollers ride up the inner rail, which draws closer to the outer one, forcing each stair to pivot upward.

How Is a Fax Sent or Received?

Facsimile, or fax, machines send text and images over phone lines. When a page is transmitted by the system below, a narrow part of the document is illuminated by a lamp, and the reflected light is directed by mirrors to a lens and a charge-coupled device (CCD). The CCD senses light and dark areas in small sections of the image band, called pixels. The pixels are digitized, or converted into numerical values that can be turned into electrical waves by a device called an analog/digital (A/D) converter. This signal is sent over phone lines by a modem. At the receiver, incoming waves are decoded and fed to a recorder, which re-creates the page from the electrical pulses using a computer-controlled thermal head made up of 1,728 wires that are rapidly heated and cooled. Where hot wires touch the paper, it changes color, creating a facsimile of the original.

Cutaway view of a fax machine

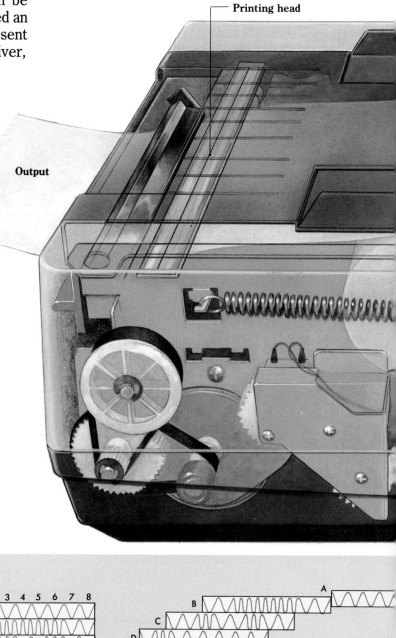

Printing head

Output

● Transmitting an image

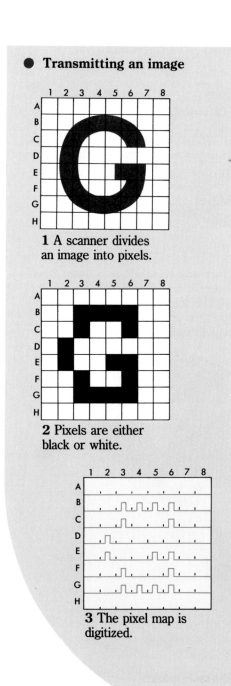

1 A scanner divides an image into pixels.

2 Pixels are either black or white.

3 The pixel map is digitized.

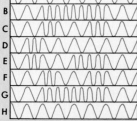

4 The digital signal is converted into an analog signal.

5 The analog signal, made up of different frequencies, is sent over the phone line.

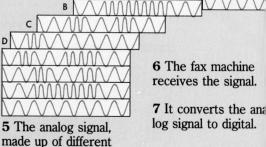

6 The fax machine receives the signal.

7 It converts the analog signal to digital.

The fax machine below sends analog, or continuous waveform, signals over the phone lines. Newer models make digital transmissions over special phone lines. These give clearer faxes and can transmit color as well as black and white.

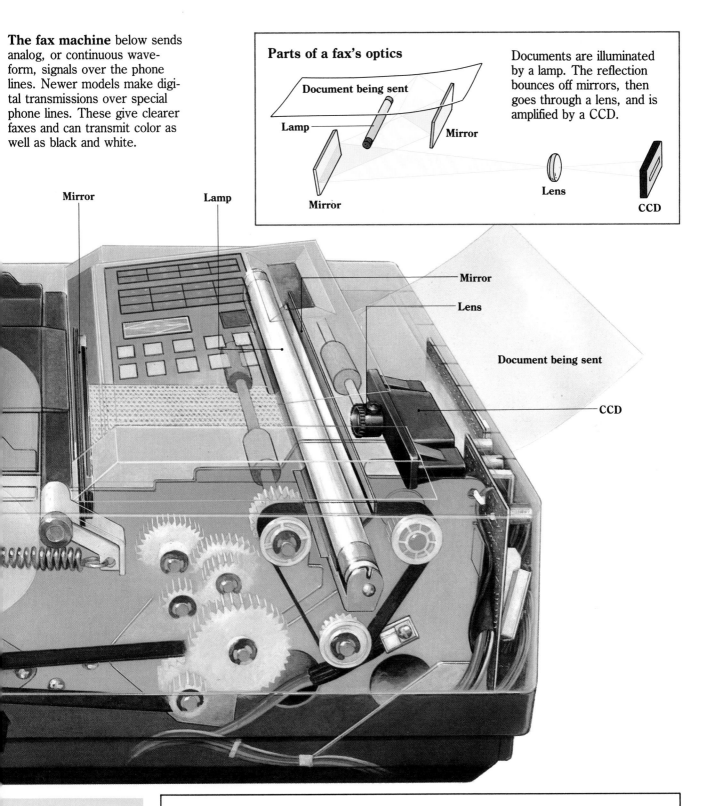

Parts of a fax's optics

Document being sent

Lamp

Mirror

Mirror

Lens

CCD

Documents are illuminated by a lamp. The reflection bounces off mirrors, then goes through a lens, and is amplified by a CCD.

Mirror

Lamp

Mirror

Lens

Document being sent

CCD

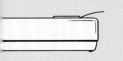

Digitized data is turned into pixels.

A pixel map reconstitutes the image.

Digital transmission

A digital fax transmits faster than the machine above. Outgoing, the CCD signal passes through an analog/digital (A/D) converter, microprocessor, and modem before it is fed to the phone line. Incoming, signals reverse the path but are sent to a printer, not the CCD.

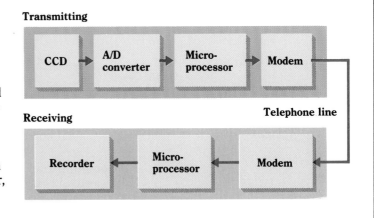

Transmitting

CCD → A/D converter → Micro-processor → Modem

Telephone line

Receiving

Recorder ← Micro-processor ← Modem

What Is an Electronic Blackboard?

Instead of slate and chalk, the electronic blackboard pairs an electronic print board with special markers, and is able to produce copies of anything sketched on its erasable surface. As one of the special markers moves across the board's surface, it causes changes in the flow of current through pressure-sensitive, conductive sheets behind the surface of the board. A few Japanese companies have pioneered these boards for use in offices and to transmit and relay information from meetings to remote branch offices.

The white surface of the board *(below)* is a thin film hiding charged, pressure-sensitive sheets.

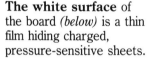

Flow on X axis

Advanced boards are linked to monitors, which offer real-time copies of what is on the board.

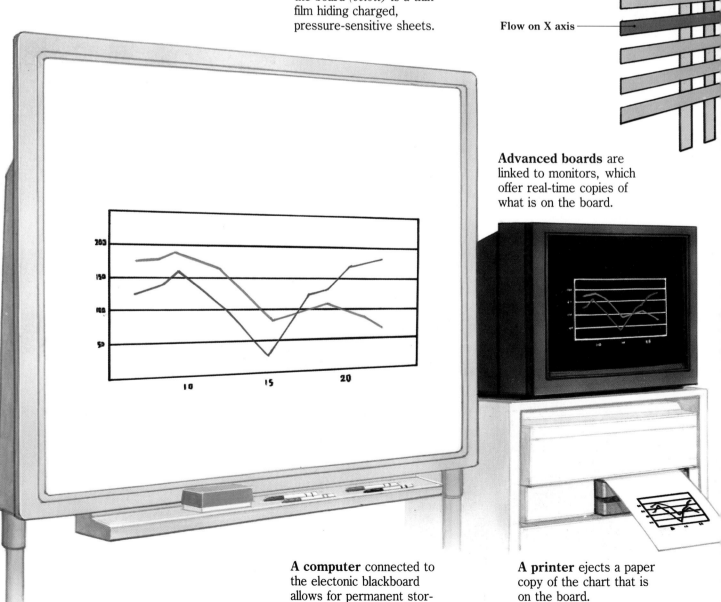

A computer connected to the electonic blackboard allows for permanent storage of the images.

A printer ejects a paper copy of the chart that is on the board.

An electronic board

Lower sheet (Y axis)

Upper sheet (X axis)

Flow on Y axis

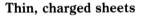

A convenient business tool

Electronic blackboards are used by some businesses in meetings. Anytime a set of figures, quickly outlined ideas, or plans need to be distributed to the participants or to other groups, the copier function can be activated.

Thin, charged sheets

The current flows at right angles in two flexible films behind the board's surface. The pressure of a pen causes the sheets to make contact, resulting in changes in the electrical resistivity at that point.

The board's sensors

locate the fluctuations in electrical resistance according to X and Y coordinates. A microprocessor translates the electrical pulses into an image using much the same method that a fax machine does.

White top surface

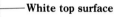

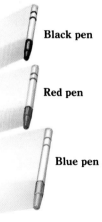

Black pen

Red pen

Blue pen

A choice of colors

The electronic blackboard recognizes three different colors of pen by means of electronic signals sent to the microprocessor when the pens are removed from holders under the board. A similar signal notifies the board that the eraser is being used.

4

Machines for Leisure Time

People at play use almost as many new machines as people in the workplace. Pictures on a television set, music on the radio, photos of friends—all rely on 20th-century inventions in electronics and chemistry.

Radio stations use electronic devices to change sounds into electrical impulses and broadcast them, and home radios change these signals back into sounds. Television stations add images to the broadcast, sending separate signals for the three colors that are reunited in a TV set.

Binoculars and all kinds of cameras—whether for photographic or for television images—rely on long-established principles of optics. This 400-year-old science deals with the ways lenses of different shapes transmit, reflect, and bend light. But recent inventions in electronics have led to such new features as autofocus, which automatically brings a photographer's subject into focus. And advances in chemistry have produced Polaroid film that develops into a photograph moments after it is exposed. Chemistry is also responsible for the special materials that make up videotapes, compact disks, and television picture tubes.

Many modern inventions have truly changed the way in which people spend their leisure time. This chapter examines the inner workings of a number of these devices that help people have fun.

A blue-and-yellow toy box overflows with electronic inventions ranging from a compact disk to movie film—a sampling of things that help make leisure time more fun. A television monitor shows how an unseen video camera views the whole scene.

How Can a Camera Focus Automatically?

A single-lens reflex camera is a tightly packed bundle of optical components and electronic circuitry. The photographer is able to focus the image manually with a twist of the focus ring around the lens, which moves the lens toward or away from the film. But a camera equipped with autofocus, called AF for short, electronically measures the distance to the subject and adjusts itself to create a perfectly focused image. One type of AF system bounces a beam of infrared light off the subject and measures the angle of its return to determine distance. Another type uses a burst of inaudible ultrasonic sound and gauges distance by timing the return of the burst. The information gathered by these AF systems causes a motor to move the lens.

A single-lens reflex camera

1 Liquid-crystal display
2 Shutter button
3 Infrared-light emitter
4 Viewing prism
5 Infrared-light detector
6 AF lens-signal contact
7 Mirror
8 Photosensor
9 Zoom lens motor
10 Mounting ring for lens
11 AF drive gear
12 AF coupler
13 Microprocessor
14 Focusing motor
15 Lens

A motor to focus the lens

When the focusing motor receives a signal from the control circuit, the motor moves the lens forward or back, into the position that brings the image into focus. A system of tiny gears makes the movement precise.

The light's path

Light goes through the lens to the mirror and splits. Some light goes through the prism to the viewfinder. The rest goes to the light sensor, or CCD, which registers the light's intensity and relays this data to the computer.

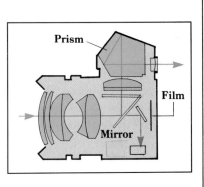

Autofocus sensor

An exploded view of the autofocus sensor module shows how light travels to the separator lenses, where the light is split to project dual images onto the CCD. When the signals are in phase, the subject is in focus.

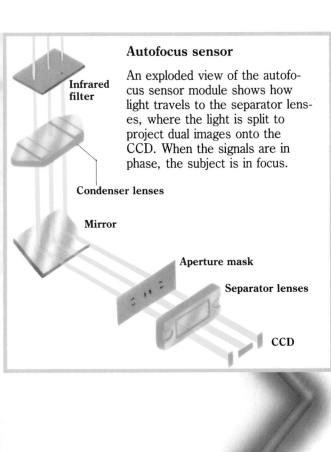

Infrared filter

Condenser lenses

Mirror

Aperture mask

Separator lenses

CCD

A chip in charge

A microprocessor *(above)* gets measurement data from the autofocusing sensor, calculates the distance to the subject, then signals the focusing motor how much to move the lens for the correct focus.

A phase-detection autofocus

As light goes through the lens, it is reflected to the separator lenses, which project dual images onto the CCD sensors. The CCDs convert the images to electrical impulses that are analyzed by the microprocessors. When these signals align with the reference signal, they are in phase and in focus.

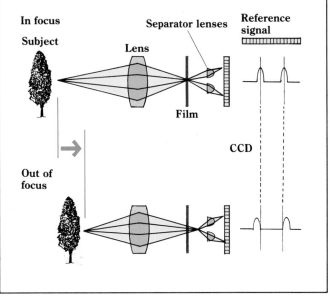

In focus

Subject

Lens

Separator lenses

Reference signal

Film

CCD

Out of focus

Different autofocus systems

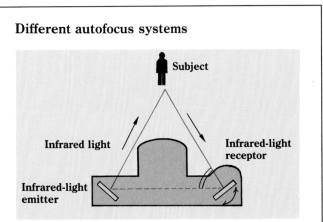

Subject

Infrared light

Infrared-light receptor

Infrared-light emitter

Infrared triangulation. In some cameras, an infrared light beam is aimed at the subject; the angle at which it returns tells the distance to the subject.

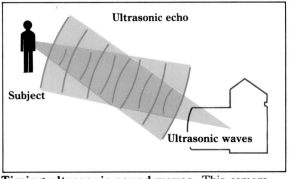

Ultrasonic echo

Subject

Ultrasonic waves

Timing ultrasonic sound waves. This camera sends out high-frequency sound waves and figures distance based on how soon the sound returns.

How Does a TV Produce Color Images?

A television screen is the flat part of a picture tube. Inside, the tube is coated with thousands of dots of phosphor—a chemical that glows when an electron hits it—arranged in 525 rows. When an electron gun at the narrow end of the tube receives signals from a TV station or a videocassette recorder, it shoots electrons at the screen. Thousands of signals per second tell the tube how brightly to light each pixel, or picture element, on the screen to form a picture. The pixels in a black-and-white picture tube can light only in white. In a color picture tube, each pixel has three kinds of phosphor—to glow red, green, or blue when hit by electrons. The tube also has three electron guns, one for each color. A television camera takes three separate pictures, one in each color. As each electron gun fires, it scans across a perforated shadow mask that allows the beam to strike only dots of the correct color. Together all the dots form one sharp image.

Structure of a color TV tube

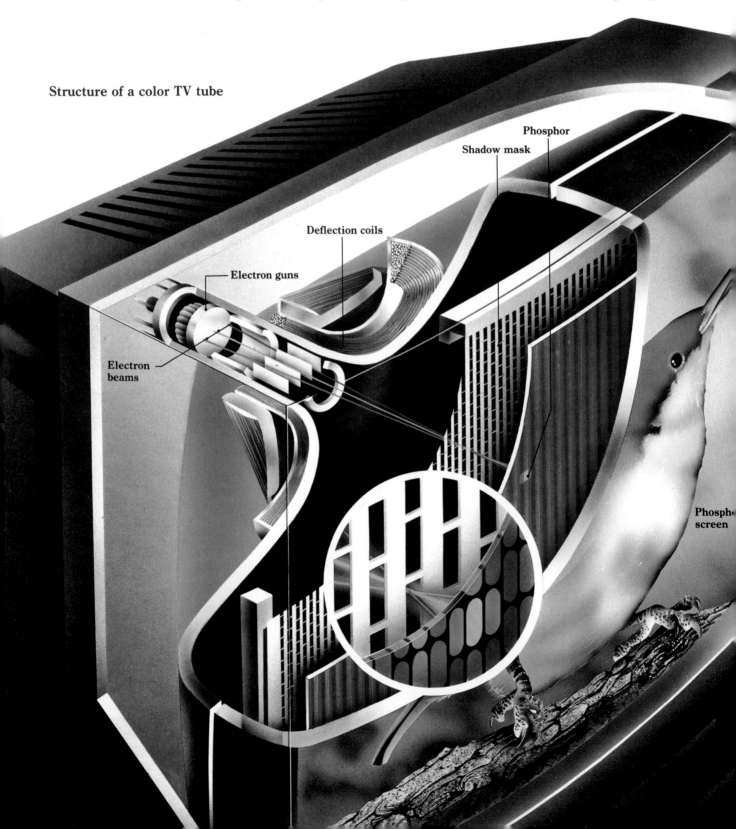

Phosphor

Shadow mask

Deflection coils

Electron guns

Electron beams

Phosphor screen

How a picture tube works

Processing signals from a TV station or VCR, electron guns shoot ordered streams of electrons at the phosphor-coated TV screen. The deflection coils direct the streams in a line from side to side, a process called scanning, to form a new picture 30 times a second.

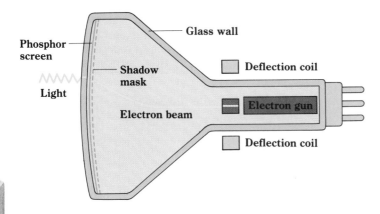

Glass wall

Phosphor screen

Shadow mask

Light

Deflection coil

Electron beam

Electron gun

Deflection coil

Scanning an image

The electron beam re-lights every other line of pixels, then goes back for the lines between. At the speed of 30 pictures per second, the eye sees no pause between pictures.

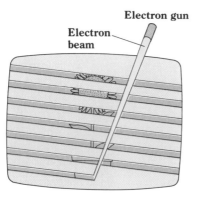

Electron gun

Electron beam

The deflection coils

The triple electron gun in a color TV picture tube stays still, but two deflection coils deflect the electrons, bending their paths as they stream toward the screen. Electricity flowing through each deflection coil creates a magnetic field. Precise variations in the magnetic fields pull the electron stream from left to right and from top to bottom, so that it covers the screen evenly. The TV signals from the station control the deflection coils.

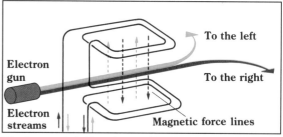

Electron gun

To the left

To the right

Electron streams

Magnetic force lines

Horizontal deflection coil

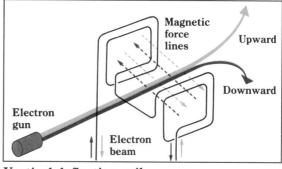

Magnetic force lines

Upward

Downward

Electron gun

Electron beam

Vertical deflection coil

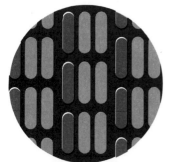

Red area of pixel

A closeup of pixels

The magnified areas below and at left match various areas of the bird on the screen opposite. To produce red, only the red phosphors are lighted; for yellow, both red and green are lighted; and for white, all three are lighted in each pixel.

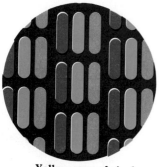

Yellow area of pixel

White area of pixel

The primary colors of light

While magenta (red), *yellow,* and cyan (blue) are the three primary colors of solid color pigments, the three primary colors of emitted light are red, *green,* and blue. The chart below shows how the three primary colors of emitted light combine to form all other colors, including white, when all three overlap.

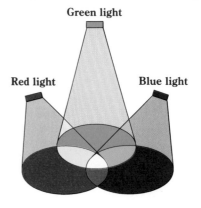

Green light

Red light

Blue light

What Is High-Definition Television?

The television systems operating in the United States and Japan use 525 lines of pixels on the picture screen. Similar systems used in Europe and elsewhere employ 625 lines. But high-definition TV being developed in Japan uses 1,125 lines, more than twice as many as the current U.S. system, on a larger screen. Because of the larger picture area, a high-definition screen is densely packed with some 2 million pixels, giving the image more detail and clarity.

One problem in the development of high-definition television is that the signal for sending the extra information for a large and detailed picture takes five times as wide a band on the frequencies available for broadcasting, which causes crowding on an already limited broadcast band. Researchers are now looking for ways to compress the high-definition signal.

More scan lines, sharper images

The high-definition picture tube *(top)* is made with 1,125 scanning lines—1,125 rows of the pixels that light up to form the images. A conventional picture tube *(bottom)*, built for the TV system now used in the United States and Japan, has fewer than half as many scan lines.

High-definition TV

Current U.S. system

Comparing system data

This table compares specifications for conventional, European, and Hi-vision television—the high-definition system being tested in Japan. All systems have a 2:1 interlace ratio, which means they scan the tube twice for each picture. But Hi-vision's proportionately wider screen uses more than twice as many scan lines.

TV system	HDTV	U.S.	Europe
Scan lines	1,125	525	625
Aspect ratio	9:16	3:4	3:4
Interlace ratio	2:1	2:1	2:1
Field frequency (Hz)	60	59.94	50
Image signal (MHz)	20	4.2	6
Audio modulation	PCM	FM	FM

Comparing picture quality

Conventional TV image

Viewing distance and field of view

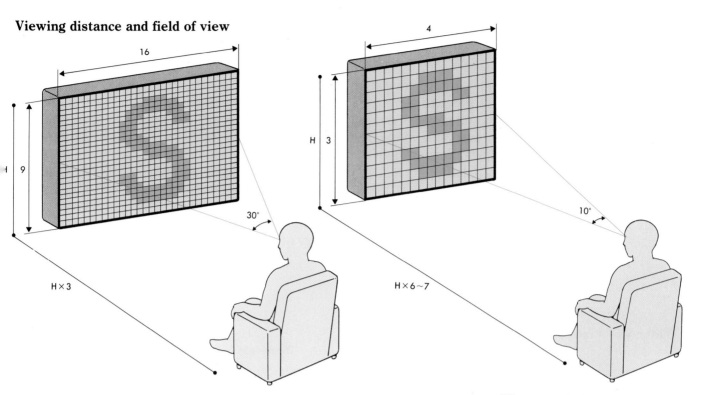

Most people like to sit far enough away from an ordinary TV to make the tube's scan lines invisible—a distance 6 or 7 times the height of the screen. A high-definition screen *(above, left)* is comfortably viewed from half as far away, and the bigger screen gives the viewer a feeling of being taken into the picture.

High-definition TV image

An image of cooking supplies looks murky and fuzzy on a conventional television screen *(left side of screen)*. On high-definition TV *(right side of screen)*, the same image looks clearer and crisper, and even lets a viewer read the labels. High-resolution TV images are almost as detailed as those made on 35-mm film.

Can a Microphone Convert Sound to Electric Signals and Back Again?

Microphones convert sound waves into electric signals, and speakers convert electric signals back into sound waves. Not surprisingly, these two instruments have several parts in common and are based on similar principles. Sound waves in the air strike a diaphragm in a dynamic microphone, making it vibrate. Small devices translate the vibrations into electric signals. When these signals reach a loudspeaker, the reverse process occurs. The signals set the speaker's diaphragm vibrating, and these vibrations generate sound waves that travel through the air to the listener's ears. Higher-pressure sound waves—that is, louder sounds—are transformed into higher-voltage electric signals in the microphone. When these are changed back into sounds, the highest-voltage pulses generate the loudest sounds in the speaker. The other important characteristic of a sound—its frequency—causes the voltage to vary at the same frequency.

Anatomy of a microphone

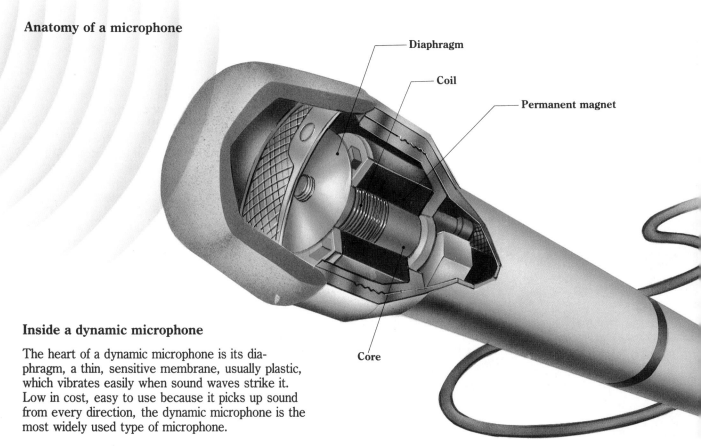

Diaphragm

Coil

Permanent magnet

Core

Inside a dynamic microphone

The heart of a dynamic microphone is its diaphragm, a thin, sensitive membrane, usually plastic, which vibrates easily when sound waves strike it. Low in cost, easy to use because it picks up sound from every direction, the dynamic microphone is the most widely used type of microphone.

How a dynamic microphone works

When sound waves hit the diaphragm, it vibrates, moving the coil connected to it. Each movement of the coil induces voltage to flow in the electromagnet around it. The voltage varies with how far the coil moves and how fast, so that the voltage pattern duplicates the sound-wave pattern in volume and frequency. The electric signals are then broadcast as electromagnetic radio waves.

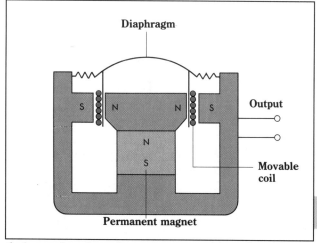

Diaphragm

S N N S

Output

Movable coil

Permanent magnet

A dynamic microphone turns sound into electricity.

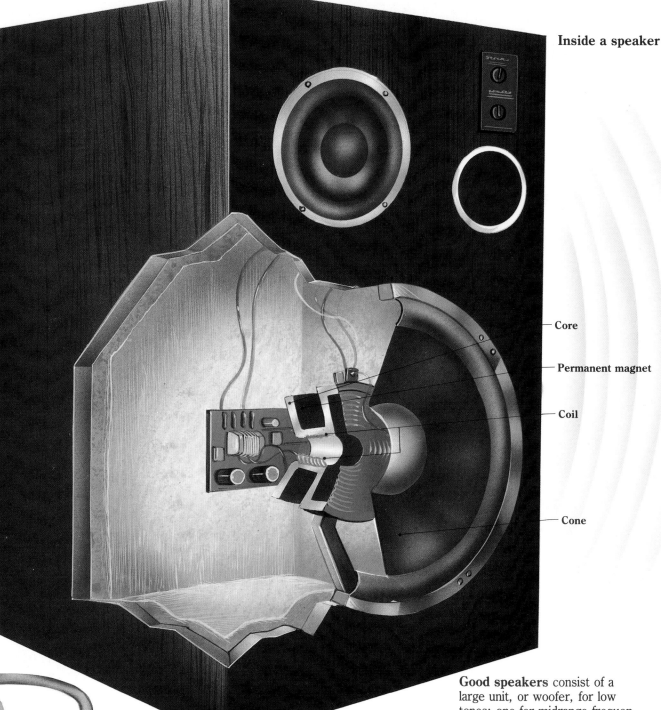

Inside a speaker

Core

Permanent magnet

Coil

Cone

Good speakers consist of a large unit, or woofer, for low tones; one for midrange frequencies; and a small speaker, or tweeter, for the high notes.

How a dynamic speaker works

A dynamic speaker is powered by a coil that lies within a circular permanent magnet. Electric signals from an amplifier come into the speaker through the input terminal. As they flow through the coil, they create a varying magnetic field, which makes the speaker's cone vibrate, forming sound waves in the air. The damper confines the vibrations to the cone, away from the rigid frame of the speaker.

Diaphragm

Direction of movement of diaphragm

Center cap

Gold wire

Speaker frame

Damper

S   N
S   N

N

S

Input terminal

Permanent magnet

Movable coil

A dynamic speaker turns electricity into sound.

How Does a VCR Record Programs?

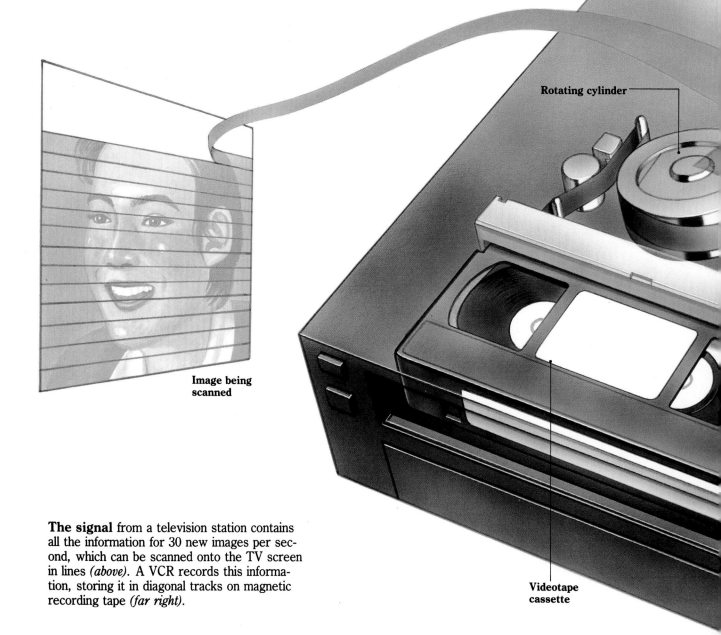

Rotating cylinder

Videotape cassette

Image being scanned

The signal from a television station contains all the information for 30 new images per second, which can be scanned onto the TV screen in lines *(above)*. A VCR records this information, storing it in diagonal tracks on magnetic recording tape *(far right)*.

A VCR, or videocassette recorder, is a machine that records television signals magnetically and plays them back by changing magnetic signals into electric signals. It stores the sound portion of a program on one track *(opposite, purple)*, reserving a much wider part of the tape for the images *(opposite, red)*. During playback, the heads pick up the signals stored in the tape, change them to electric signals, and send them to a TV set.

The visual portion of a program signal carries 30 images per second. To record this much information, the recorder uses two video heads. These are mounted inside the video head drum *(opposite, blue circle)*, spinning at 30 revolutions per second. With each revolution, the two heads record one complete television-screen image on the tape as it moves past the drum. Signals previously recorded on the tape have been erased by an erasing head before the tape reaches the video recording heads. The heads record new signals by rearranging the magnetic particles in the recording tape *(opposite, bottom)*, into new patterns.

Meanwhile, the sound portion of the signal is recorded by a separate audio recording head, next to a head that erases the old soundtrack.

A videocassette recorder

How the image is recorded

The recording drum is mounted at an angle, so that the tape moves across it diagonally and the recorded tracks appear in diagonal strips across the tape. This method gets the most information possible on each inch of tape.

Image being played back

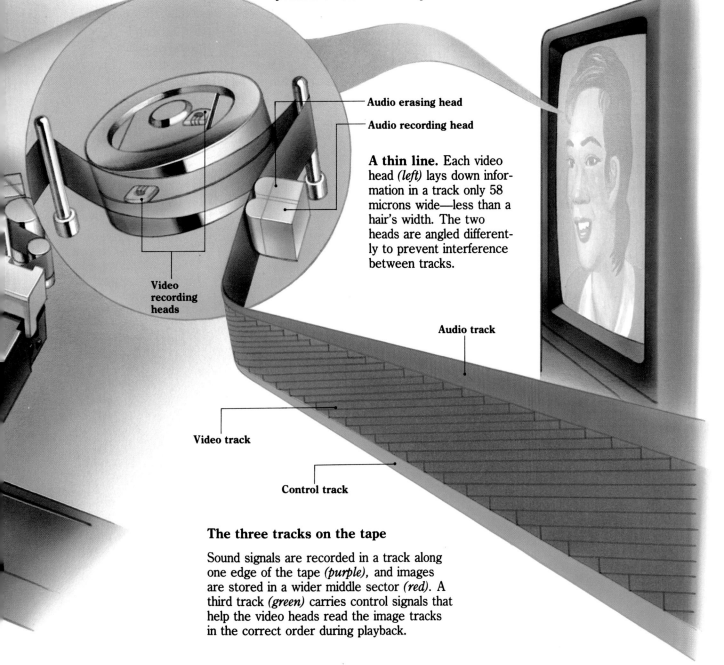

Audio erasing head

Audio recording head

A thin line. Each video head *(left)* lays down information in a track only 58 microns wide—less than a hair's width. The two heads are angled differently to prevent interference between tracks.

Video recording heads

Audio track

Video track

Control track

The three tracks on the tape

Sound signals are recorded in a track along one edge of the tape *(purple),* and images are stored in a wider middle sector *(red).* A third track *(green)* carries control signals that help the video heads read the image tracks in the correct order during playback.

How magnetic recording works

Inside the recording-and-playback head, signal current flows through the coil, inducing a varying magnetic field in the electromagnet. As the recording tape moves past the gap in the electromagnet, the tiny metallic particles in the tape are magnetized in turn by the magnetic pulses, encoding the signal's pattern on the tape. The recording stays on the tape until new magnetic signals erase it.

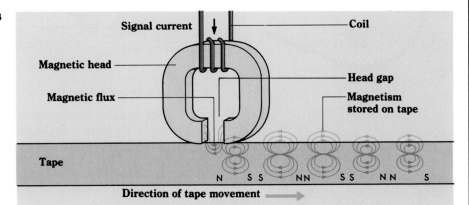

Signal current

Coil

Magnetic head

Head gap

Magnetic flux

Magnetism stored on tape

Tape

N   S S   NN   S S   N N   S

Direction of tape movement →

How Does a Radio Transmit Sound?

Every radio program first exists as sound waves—patterned movements in air—which microphones change into patterned electrical signals. From atop the station's tall metal antenna, these electrical signals are broadcast as electromagnetic waves, which travel invisibly through air and space at the speed of light. Like all waves, radio waves are described by frequency—the number of times the signal varies from strong to weak and back again in a second—and by amplitude—their height. All AM stations put their program signals onto a carrier signal at an assigned frequency.

Many radio waves reach radios, but the tuner picks out one carrier frequency at a time. The weak electrical radio waves detected by the antenna must then be made stronger, or amplified, and the carrier signal must be filtered out from the program signal. The remaining waves are in the same frequency range as sound and are sent to the speakers, which vibrate to produce the sound.

Turning radio waves into sound

Tuning circuit

Tuning

A radio antenna captures radio waves from many sources "on the air." Turning the AM dial adjusts the tuner to receive only radio signals of a particular station's carrier frequency.

Radio frequency amplifier

Program and carrier signals mixed

Carrying a signal

The variable signals that are the program are carried on the back of the constant wave-form that is the carrier wave *(above)*. Together, these waves go through the radio frequency amplifier and are amplified, or made taller.

Anatomy of a radio

Coil

Variable capacitor

Speaker

Battery

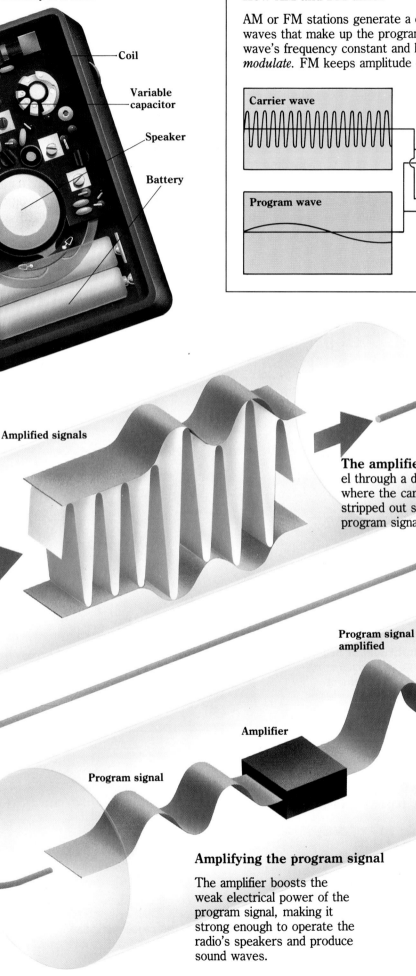

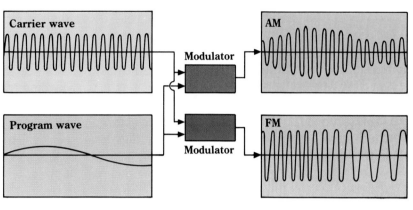

How AM and FM differ

AM or FM stations generate a carrier wave on which to transmit the waves that make up the program. But an AM transmitter keeps its wave's frequency constant and lets the *amplitude* of program signals *modulate*. FM keeps amplitude constant but *modulates frequency*.

Carrier wave

Program wave

Modulator

Modulator

AM

FM

Amplified signals

Demodulator

The amplified waves travel through a demodulator, where the carrier wave is stripped out so that only the program signal will move on.

Program signal amplified

Amplifier

Program signal

Converting to sound

In the speaker, the patterned electrical signals form a magnetic field, whose variations make the speaker vibrate, re-creating the sound waves of the original radio program.

Amplifying the program signal

The amplifier boosts the weak electrical power of the program signal, making it strong enough to operate the radio's speakers and produce sound waves.

Why Do Compact Disks Sound So Clear?

A compact disk, with its tightly spiraling track reflecting light in rainbow colors *(opposite)*, can record a wider range of sounds than a phonograph record, with almost no distortion. One reason for this quality is that the CD's playing surface is protected by a plastic layer. Unlike a phonograph record, the disk is never touched by a stylus and cannot be scratched. Instead it is read by a tightly focused laser beam.

To be stored on a CD, sounds must first be converted from analog wave-forms to their digital, or stepped, equivalents *(below, center),* so

that they can be represented in binary code. This coded sequence of *0*'s and *1*'s then becomes a pattern of tiny pits etched on a plastic disk. The disk is coated with a thin layer of aluminum, which reflects light. Scanned by a laser beam from below—through the plastic covering—the pits scatter the light that hits them. A CD's recording track starts near the middle and runs out to the edge in a tight spiral of 100,000 turns to an inch. The track is far narrower than a hair and several miles long. During playback, the disk spins as fast as 500 times per minute.

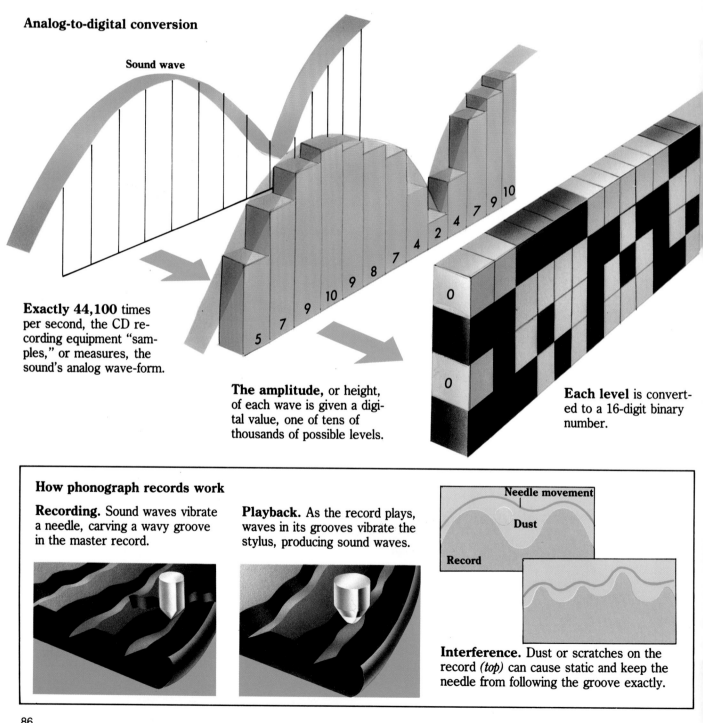

Analog-to-digital conversion

Sound wave

Exactly 44,100 times per second, the CD recording equipment "samples," or measures, the sound's analog wave-form.

The amplitude, or height, of each wave is given a digital value, one of tens of thousands of possible levels.

Each level is converted to a 16-digit binary number.

How phonograph records work

Recording. Sound waves vibrate a needle, carving a wavy groove in the master record.

Playback. As the record plays, waves in its grooves vibrate the stylus, producing sound waves.

Needle movement

Dust

Record

Interference. Dust or scratches on the record *(top)* can cause static and keep the needle from following the groove exactly.

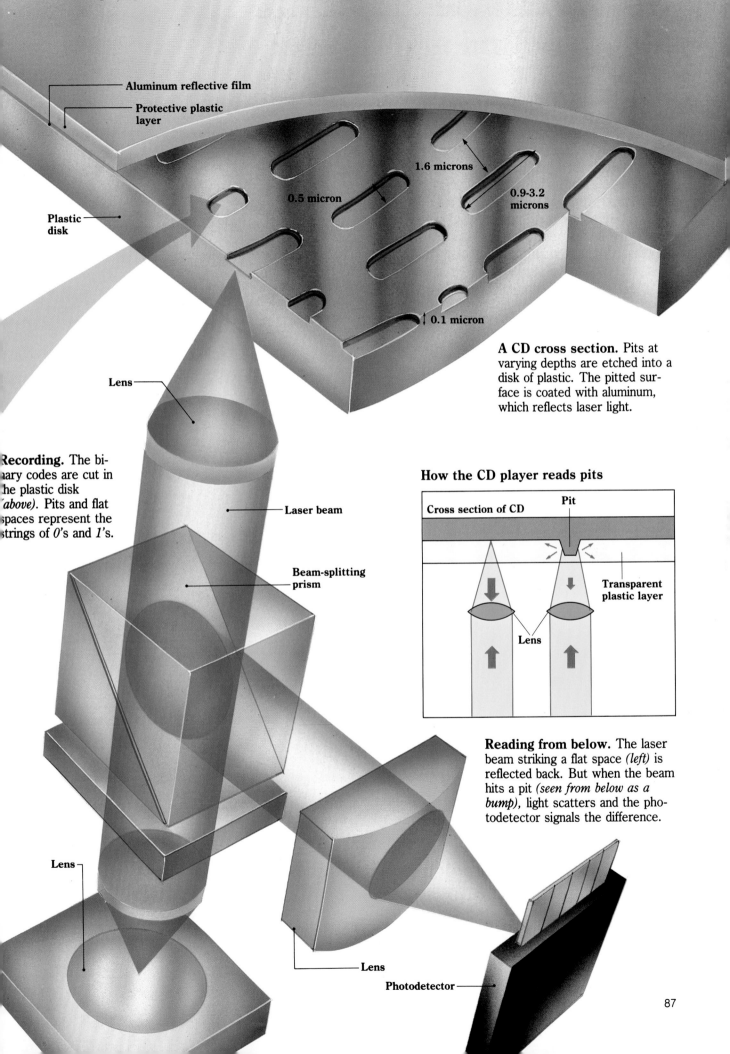

CD and laser pickup

Aluminum reflective film

Protective plastic layer

Plastic disk

1.6 microns

0.5 micron

0.9-3.2 microns

0.1 micron

A CD cross section. Pits at varying depths are etched into a disk of plastic. The pitted surface is coated with aluminum, which reflects laser light.

Lens

Recording. The binary codes are cut in the plastic disk *(above)*. Pits and flat spaces represent the strings of *0*'s and *1*'s.

Laser beam

Beam-splitting prism

How the CD player reads pits

Cross section of CD

Pit

Transparent plastic layer

Lens

Reading from below. The laser beam striking a flat space *(left)* is reflected back. But when the beam hits a pit *(seen from below as a bump)*, light scatters and the photodetector signals the difference.

Lens

Lens

Photodetector

How Do Movie Projectors Match Sound and Image?

A movie projector, such as the model shown below, works by shining light through images on film and then through a lens that focuses the images on a screen. Gears with sprockets move the film one frame at a time, 24 frames per second. Meanwhile, a rotating shutter in front of the lens lets light shine twice through each frame and cuts off light as the next frame moves into place *(opposite, top)*. Sound for each frame is recorded along one edge of the film, several frames away. As each image is projected, its matching sound is read off the film by the sound drum a few inches away. Thus the sound from the speaker always matches the action on the screen.

Anatomy of a movie projector

Inside the sound drum

A movie's soundtrack may be converted to pulses of light and laid down on the film. In the projector's sound drum *(below)*, the light of an exciter lamp, focused through a lens, goes through the soundtrack and onto a photocell, which reconverts the pulses into electric signals. These signals are amplified and sent to the speaker. Film sound may also be recorded magnetically.

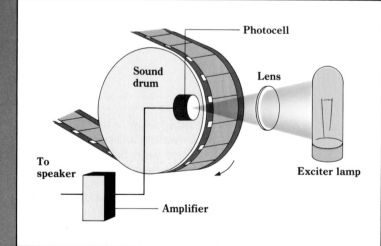

- Photocell
- Sound drum
- Lens
- To speaker
- Exciter lamp
- Amplifier

1 Lamp housing
2 Sprocket
3 Aperture
4 Projection lens
5 Changeover lever
6 Sound lens
7 Exciter lamp
8 Magnetic recording/playback head
9 Sound drum

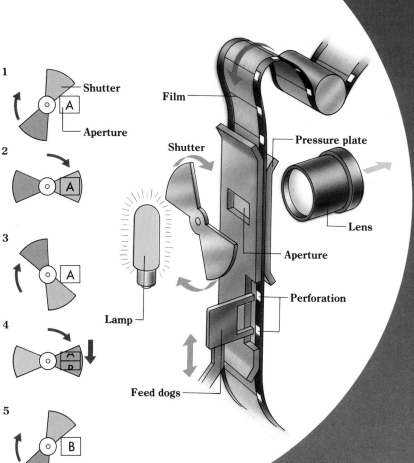

The rotating shutter

The two-bladed rotating shutter, turning in front of the projector's aperture, lets two pulses of light shine through each frame of the film (1-3). The blade also blocks the light (4) while the film advances to the next frame (5). The film moves at 24 frames per second, but because the screen is relighted 48 times per second, human eyes see no flickering.

1

Shutter

A

Aperture

2

A

3

A

4

5

B

Film

Shutter

Pressure plate

Lens

Aperture

Perforation

Lamp

Feed dogs

Sending light through the film

Light from the projection bulb shines through the film, aperture window, and lens, and through the gaps in the rotating shutter, which is open only when a frame is in position for viewing.

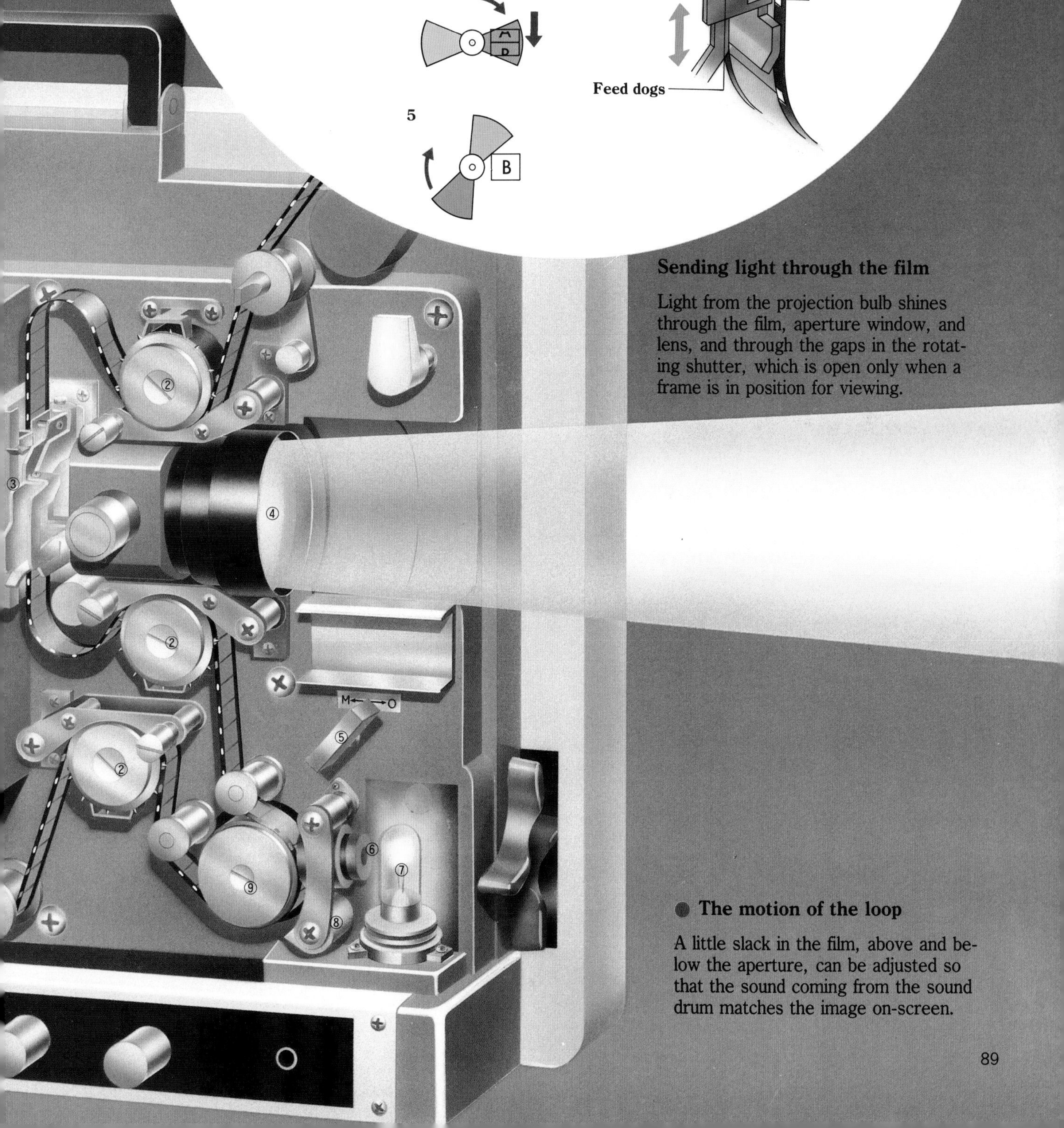

M ← → O

● The motion of the loop

A little slack in the film, above and below the aperture, can be adjusted so that the sound coming from the sound drum matches the image on-screen.

What Is a Synthesizer?

A sound synthesizer uses computer technology to imitate musical instruments by controlling the quality of the sounds it produces. Every sound has pitch, timbre, and loudness. Pitch depends on a sound's frequency in waves per second. Timbre depends on the shape of the wave. Loudness depends on amplitude: Louder sounds have taller waves. Another quality of a sound, called its envelope *(bottom green diagram),* determines how the sound changes while it exists. How fast does loudness grow at its onset, and how fast does it fade? Each kind of sound has a distinctive envelope. The synthesizer generates sounds with various kinds of voltage control (VC). The key that has been struck tells the VC oscillator (VCO) to emit voltage at a given frequency. The VC filter (VCF) alters the wave-form, the VC amplifier (VCA) adjusts average loudness, and the envelope generator (EG) makes complex changes in loudness in the short term.

■ **Basic parts of a synthesizer**

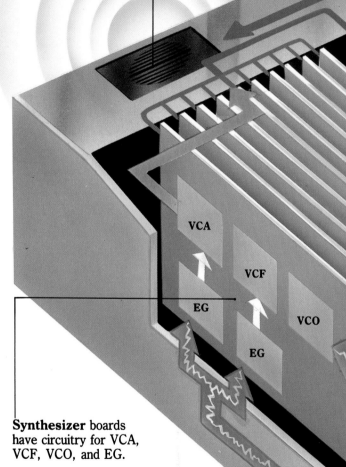

Speaker

VC oscillator

The pitch of a sound depends on the frequency of the wave. The oscillator generates sounds of different frequencies.

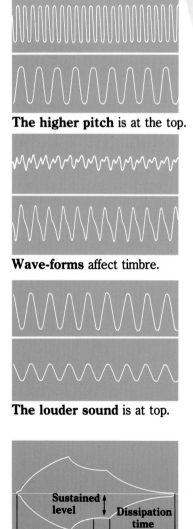

The higher pitch is at the top.

VC filter

Different wave-forms give each sound its distinctive timbre. The filter adds timbre by altering the forms, making them sound like notes from a musical instrument.

Wave-forms affect timbre.

VC amplifier

A sound's loudness depends on the height of the wave, which the amplifier varies, and is relative to how hard the keys have been struck.

The louder sound is at top.

Synthesizer boards have circuitry for VCA, VCF, VCO, and EG.

Envelope generator

The EG acts on the VCF and the VCA to make a series of changes in a sound's loudness as the sound rises rapidly, steadies to a sustained level, and dies away.

Sustained level
Dissipation time
Rise time
Sustained time
Attenuation time

Amplitude is charted over time.

When the player strikes a key, voltage for that note enters the VCO, which generates sound-source signals of a fundamental tone and its related overtones. The VCF reshapes the wave-form, removing unwanted components from the signal, and sends it to the VCA to be amplified. As the sound emerges, its wave-form and loudness change over time according to how the key was struck and how the EG is set.

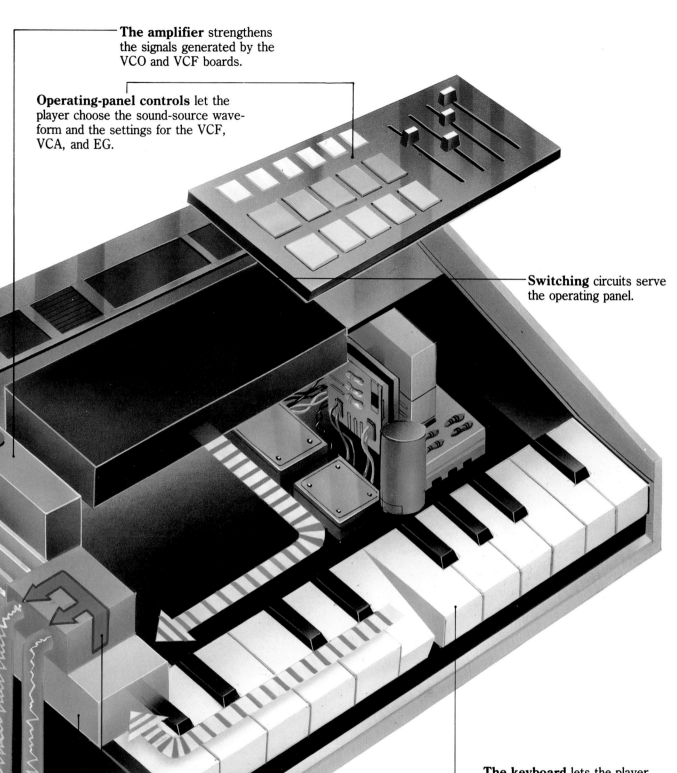

The amplifier strengthens the signals generated by the VCO and VCF boards.

Operating-panel controls let the player choose the sound-source wave-form and the settings for the VCF, VCA, and EG.

Switching circuits serve the operating panel.

The keyboard lets the player pick the sequence and timing.

The digital-to-analog converter changes digital signals to analog signals and sends them to the circuitry boards.

The computer receives digital signals when the player sets the controls and strikes the keys.

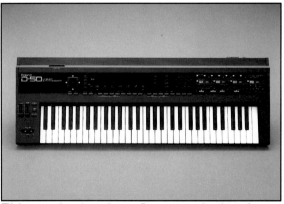

This synthesizer has a five-octave keyboard.

How Are Instant Color Photos Made?

A sheet of instant film is a nine-layer sandwich of chemicals between an opaque black bottom and a transparent top *(opposite)*. It contains a packet of developing fluid as well as three light-sensitive emulsions—one layer to absorb blue light, one for green, and one for red. Each light-sensitive layer is paired with a layer of dye in its complementary color.

When light strikes the film, each of the three light-sensitive layers absorbs only its specific color of light. Immediately after exposure the film is pushed through rollers out of the camera. The roller pressure bursts the sealed packet of developer and floods the light-sensitive layers with developer. Everywhere light has been absorbed the developer turns silver compounds in the light-sensitive layers into crystals of silver; these crystals block the release of dye in that layer. The dyes in the unexposed layers, however, are the colors that match the color of light that struck that area, and they are free to migrate to the top layer of the film, forming the image.

4 **The finished photo.** The chemical process is complete, and the image is formed, about a minute after the picture is snapped.

3 **Color migration.** Where green light struck the green-sensitive layer *(below),* the developer forms a silver layer, and blocks the magenta dye. But the yellow and cyan dyes rise into the film's image area and mix to make green. Yellow and magenta mix for red, and cyan and magenta for purple.

Subtracting color from light

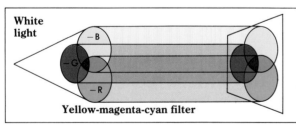

White
light

Yellow-magenta-cyan filter

White light combines all colors of the spectrum. Subtracting, or blocking, a color from white light lets other colors come through. By this method, yellow filters absorb blue, magenta absorbs green, and cyan absorbs red. If mixed in the right proportions, any color can be produced. Where all three filters overlap, all colors are blocked, and the result is black.

Making instant images

Polaroid optics

As in any camera, the lens in an instant camera reverses the image it projects. A mirror at the back of the camera reflects the image onto the film *(left)*. Each color of light from the image penetrates the layers of the film to a different depth *(below)*.

Film

1 Exposure. The light from the subject strikes silver crystals in the three sensitive emulsions.

2 Development. After the shutter closes, the motor pushes the film out between rollers. Developer in the film is squeezed over the image area and goes to work releasing dyes, except where exposed silver compounds block them.

Clear plastic layer

Positive print layer

Blue-sensitized emulsion

Yellow developer layer

Green-sensitized emulsion

Magenta developer layer

Red-sensitized emulsion

Cyan developer layer

Opaque black base

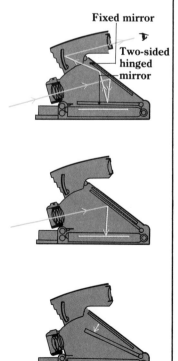

Taking a picture

Focusing. The hinged two-sided mirror lies flat, reflecting light to the viewfinder, as the photographer focuses.

Fixed mirror

Two-sided hinged mirror

Exposing. When the shutter is released, the two-sided mirror flips up, exposing the film to the light.

Ejecting. As the rollers eject the film, the viewfinder mirror drops back into place.

93

How Do Binoculars Magnify Objects?

Binoculars, the second most popular optical device after cameras, add enjoyment to sports and concerts by allowing more details to be seen. A pair of binoculars also provides a degree of depth perception that a telescope's single eyepiece cannot. The most widely used design relies on convex lenses *(bottom, right)*.

Since a convex lens reverses the image—both up for down and left for right—a set of prisms corrects the inversions. Going through these prisms, the light is reflected four times as it passes from the objective lens to the eyepiece. Because of these reflections, the light takes a long path across a short distance, so the tube needed for binoculars can be made much shorter than that for telescopes.

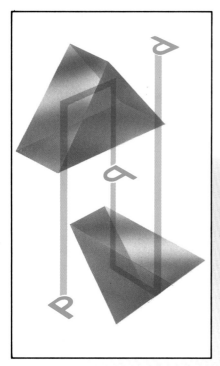

The prisms

Built into the optical path—the light's path in the binoculars—the first prism flops images left for right, and the second turns them right side up, correcting inversions.

Eyepiece

Prisms

■ Magnifying distant objects

The largest binoculars magnify images up to 35 times life size. The more popular midsize binoculars magnify 6 to 7 times and give a bright image, making them suitable for bird watching or bringing any scene closer. A rating of 7 x 50 means magnification of 7 times and an objective lens diameter of 50 mm.

Objective lens

● Binocular optics

The objective lens brings an image into focus in the optical path. The lens at the eyepiece creates a virtual image, providing an enlarged view.

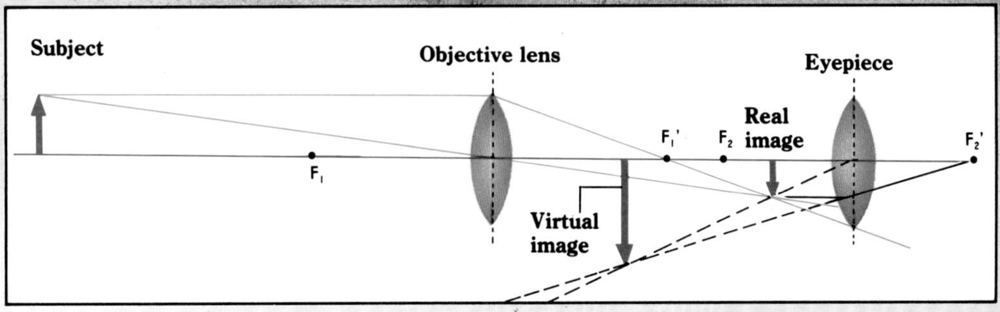

Subject   **Objective lens**   **Eyepiece**

F_1' F_2 **Real image** F_2'

F_1

Virtual image

Why Is Quartz Used in Watches?

Certain crystals, called piezoelectric substances, produce electric current when compressed. Conversely, applying electric current to a piezoelectric crystal changes its shape slightly. This change is not simply one distorting bulge; the crystal oscillates, or swings back and forth, at a rate that stays the same from one second to the next. Quartz is one such piezoelectric substance and is used as a timekeeper in clocks and watches. Quartz can be made to oscillate, under electric current, at a precise frequency. Microchip circuitry can convert that frequency to precisely one vibration per second. This unvarying natural oscillation gives quartz-powered clocks and watches accuracy that no mechanical timepiece could ever match.

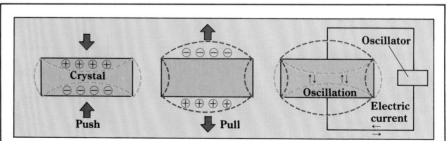

Battery

A natural quartz crystal

Structure of quartz

Quartz is a colorless, transparent crystal of silicon dioxide. Its silicon and oxygen atoms are joined by ionic bonds, which means they are held together by opposing electrical charges.

A unit cell shows the structure of quartz, with silicon atoms *(purple)* bonding with oxygen atoms *(green)*.

How piezoelectricity occurs

Under pressure, piezoelectric crystals produce electricity. This occurs because deforming the crystal *(right)* breaks some ionic bonds and releases electrons, forming a positive charge on one side and a negative on the other.

Oscillator

Crystal

Oscillation

Electric current

Push

Pull

Pulses. Pressure *(left)* forms electrical charges on opposite sides of the crystal. A pull *(middle)* reverses the charges. And so a stream of positive and negative charges *(right)* makes the crystal pulsate.

Anatomy of a quartz watch

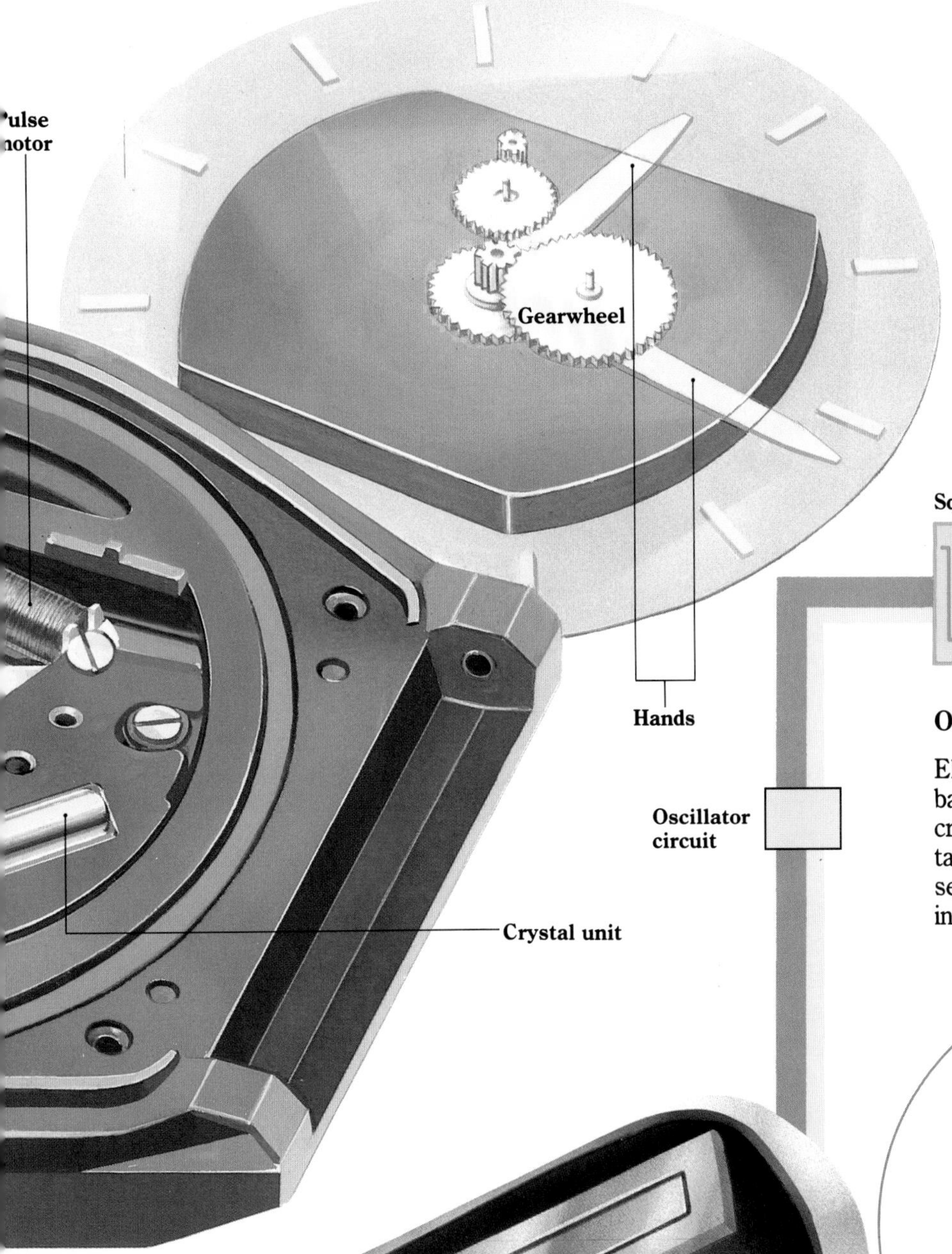

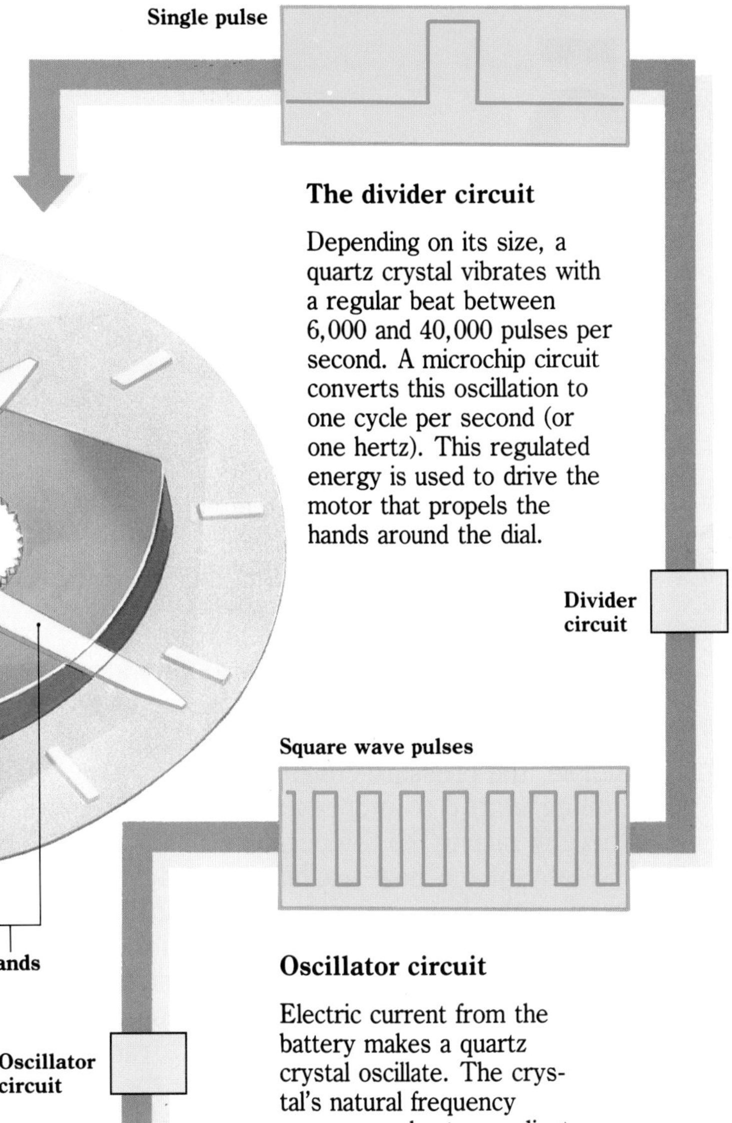

The divider circuit

Depending on its size, a quartz crystal vibrates with a regular beat between 6,000 and 40,000 pulses per second. A microchip circuit converts this oscillation to one cycle per second (or one hertz). This regulated energy is used to drive the motor that propels the hands around the dial.

Divider circuit

Square wave pulses

Oscillator circuit

Electric current from the battery makes a quartz crystal oscillate. The crystal's natural frequency serves as a beat, coordinating all parts of the circuit.

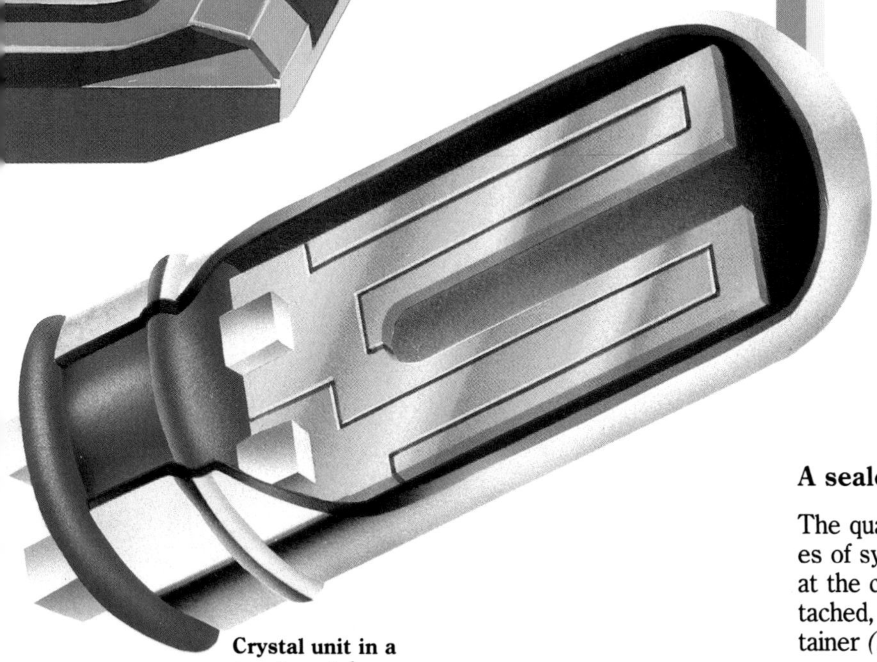

Pulse motor

Gearwheel

Hands

Oscillator circuit

Crystal unit

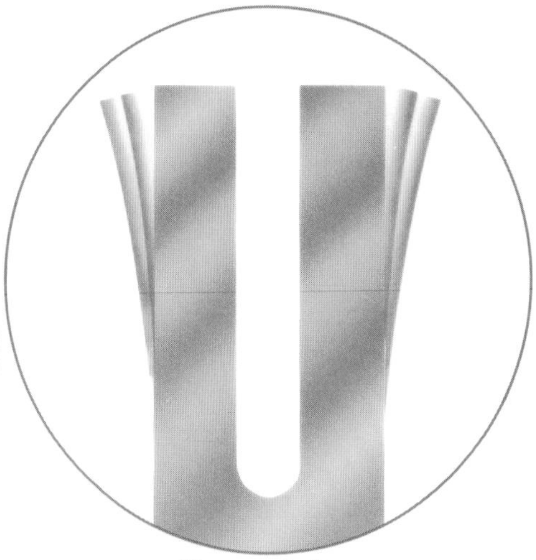

Movement of a quartz oscillator

A sealed quartz oscillator

The quartz oscillator *(above)* is made with thin slices of synthetic quartz, shaped so it will resonate at the chosen frequency. Electrical leads are attached, and the assembly, sealed in an airless container *(left)*, becomes a watch's crystal unit.

Crystal unit in a quartz watch

5

Machines for the Home

More than just a place to sleep, home is a place to cook meals, sew and wash clothes, take a bath, or simply relax in comfort. More and more of these activities involve new machines. Some of the many devices used in the home depend on principles understood since ancient times. The water faucet is an adaptation of one of the simplest and earliest machines, the screw. Equally simple, the pressure cooker clamps a lid on boiling water to increase the pressure, thereby raising the temperature.

Many of the new machines and devices used in the home operate electronically—and automatically. That is, they turn themselves on or off in response to sensors or timers. A refrigerator keeps the foods inside cooled to a given temperature range and turns on its cooling cycle when the inside warms up. An electric iron stays within a chosen temperature range because a heat sensor cuts off the current when the maximum temperature is reached. A clothes washer performs its wash-drain-rinse-spin cycles in accord with a timer. A security system—perhaps the ultimate in sensors—relies on devices sensitive to intrusion. This chapter examines the principles and mechanisms at work inside some of the machines that enhance life in the home.

Many inventions for the home, ranging from the simple faucet to the complex microwave oven, make life easier, safer, and more comfortable.

Can More Pressure Speed Up Cooking?

A pressure cooker is a piece of applied physics for the kitchen. The pot makes use of the fact that water boils at different temperatures, depending on the surrounding pressure. The air pressure at sea level is known as 1 atmosphere. Water heated at that pressure boils at 212° F. When boiling starts, bubbles form in the water as some of the water turns from liquid to gas and escapes as steam. This process is called a phase change. Once the water has reached a full boil, additional heat does not raise the water's temperature, but turns it to steam instead. In a sealed pressure cooker, however, the pressure may equal 2 atmospheres. At this pressure, the phase change from water to steam occurs not at 212° F., but at 266° F., which allows food to cook in one-third the usual time. So a pressure cooker could be called a high-temperature cooker; the increased pressure permits the higher temperatures.

Screw-dov
knob

Deadweight valve

Spring to hold arm

Rubber gasket

Air pressure and boiling point

As this chart shows, high air pressure raises water's boiling point. At low pressure—below 1 atmosphere—as in the mountains, water boils at lower temperatures and foods take longer to cook. Under higher pressure, water must reach a higher temperature before it can boil.

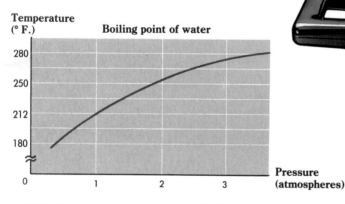

Temperature (° F.)

Boiling point of water

280
250
212
180

0   1   2   3

Pressure (atmospheres)

Soup pot versus pressure cooker

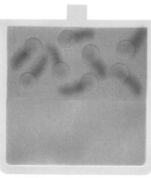

Water molecules

A pot often has thin sides and a loose-fitting lid. Steam escapes from the boiling water, and the temperature cannot rise above 212° F.

A pressure cooker has thick walls, an airtight lid, and valves to control pressure. Heating raises pressure and temperature.

Pressure-cooker anatomy

To resist the pressures that build up during cooking, a pressure cooker *(below)* needs sturdy walls and a lid that fastens securely in place. Three devices *(right)*—the dead-weight valve, the safety valve, and the gasket—are designed to keep the pressure in the pot under accurate control.

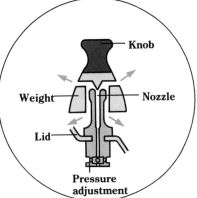

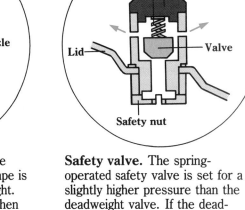

Deadweight valve. The hole through which steam can escape is blocked from above by a weight. Steam is released in bursts when its pressure lifts the weight.

Safety valve. The spring-operated safety valve is set for a slightly higher pressure than the deadweight valve. If the dead-weight valve jams, pressure opens the safety valve.

Rubber gasket. If both the dead-weight valve and safety valve should fail, the rubber gasket gives way *(left),* letting steam escape to prevent a buildup of pressure that could cause the pot to explode.

Support arm

Lid

Clamp

Sealing the pressure cooker

Turning the handle raises the support arm into place under the clamps and presses the lid down into position against the gasket around the rim of the pot.

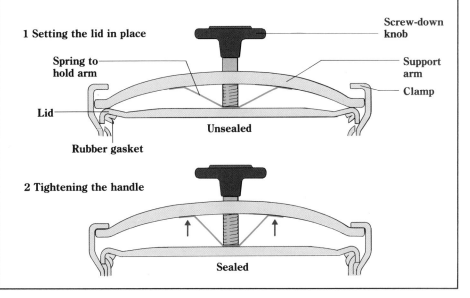

1 Setting the lid in place

Screw-down knob

Spring to hold arm

Support arm

Clamp

Lid

Rubber gasket

Unsealed

2 Tightening the handle

Sealed

What Causes Microwaves to Cook Food?

A microwave oven cooks not with heat but with radiation similar to radar waves. The heat in an ordinary oven first hits the outside of a food and works its way inward. But microwave radiation goes through the food, bounces off the floor or wall of the oven, and goes through the food again.

Microwave radiation also changes its polarity, or its positive-negative direction, several billion times a second. The rapidly oscillating microwave radiation acts on the water in food because of a special property of water. Water molecules also have polarity. Made up of one oxygen atom, which is negative, and two hydrogen atoms, which are positive, each water molecule has a positive and a negative end. Every water molecule responds to the reversal of the microwave field by reversing itself *(diagrams below)*, twisting back and forth billions of times a second. As the twisting water molecules rub against other molecules, they generate friction, which causes the food to heat up and cook rapidly.

A magnetron

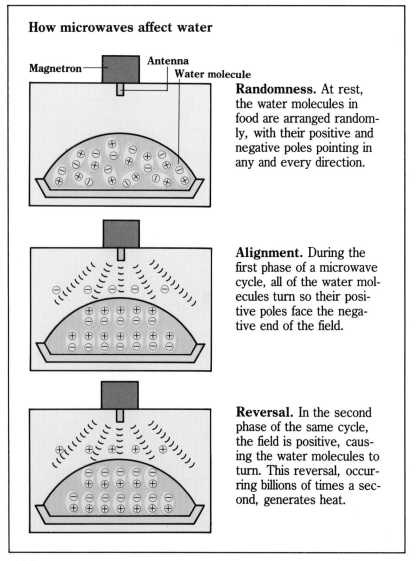

How microwaves affect water

Magnetron — Antenna
Water molecule

Randomness. At rest, the water molecules in food are arranged randomly, with their positive and negative poles pointing in any and every direction.

Alignment. During the first phase of a microwave cycle, all of the water molecules turn so their positive poles face the negative end of the field.

Reversal. In the second phase of the same cycle, the field is positive, causing the water molecules to turn. This reversal, occurring billions of times a second, generates heat.

How a magnetron makes waves

The key fixture in a microwave oven is a magnetron, a type of electron tube, which generates electrons from a heated cathode. The cathode's outer surface consists of electron-emitting materials, which produce a cascade of electrons when the cathode is heated with a flow of thousands of volts of direct current. The cathode is the negative pole, surrounded by a ring-shaped positive anode, which contains a number of resonance chambers. The cathode and the anode are sandwiched between two permanent magnets. If the magnitudes of the electric field and the magnetic field are properly adjusted, the electrons issuing from the cathode move in a direction roughly perpendicular to both fields. These movements set up a traveling wave that rotates and resonates in synchronism with the electrons in the space between the cathode and the anode, converting the electrons' power to microwave energy.

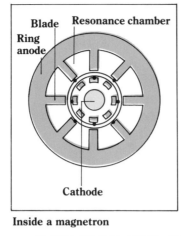

Blade **Resonance chamber**
Ring anode
Cathode

Inside a magnetron

Cooking in a microwave oven

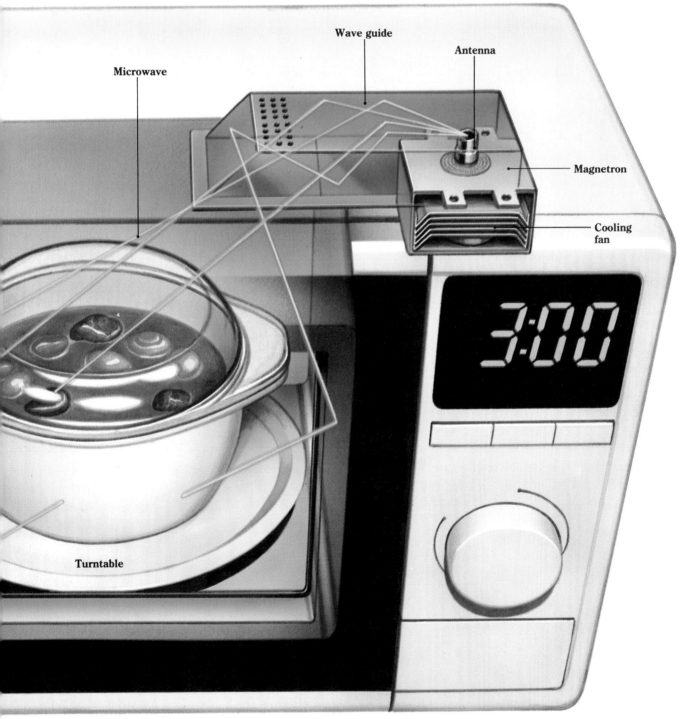

Microwave

Wave guide

Antenna

Magnetron

Cooling fan

Turntable

How Can a Machine Sew?

A sewing machine forms stitches by using not one thread but two. One thread is applied from above the fabric by the needle, and the other one comes from a small spool, called a bobbin, below the fabric. The machine makes each stitch by looping one thread through the other with a rotating shuttle *(opposite, bottom)*, then pulling the loop tight from above with the take-up lever *(opposite)*. Once a stitch is completed, a toothed plate known as the feed dog, located in the machine base just under the needle, pushes the fabric into position for the next stitch.

All these devices—needle, shuttle, take-up lever, and feed dog—are linked by gears to the same power source and work in synchronization, each doing its part in turn. The first sewing machines were driven by a hand-turned crank or a foot-operated treadle. Now an electric motor provides the power. Some sewing machines also have a microprocessor, programmed to move the needle in many special patterns *(opposite)*.

How the needle moves

The needle must go up and down for every stitch, but it can also go sideways for short distances. When the needle moves to the left and right while sewing, it produces a zigzag seam.

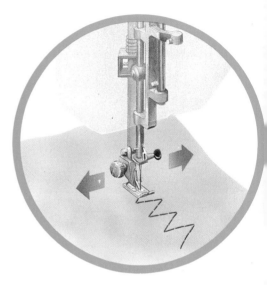

How the feed dog moves fabric

To move the fabric ahead in the direction of the wide green arrow *(right)*, the feed dog moves up and forward *(small green arrows)*, sliding the fabric along under the presser foot. While the stitch is made, the feed dog drops down and back to get a new grip. The stitch-size setting controls how far the feed dog moves.

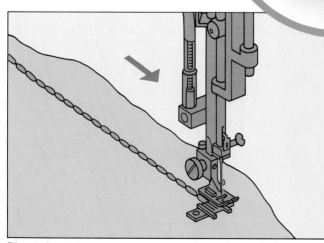

Short feed-dog movements produce short stitches.

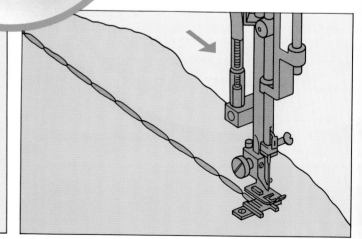

Long stitches result when feed dog slides fabric farther.

A computerized sewing machine

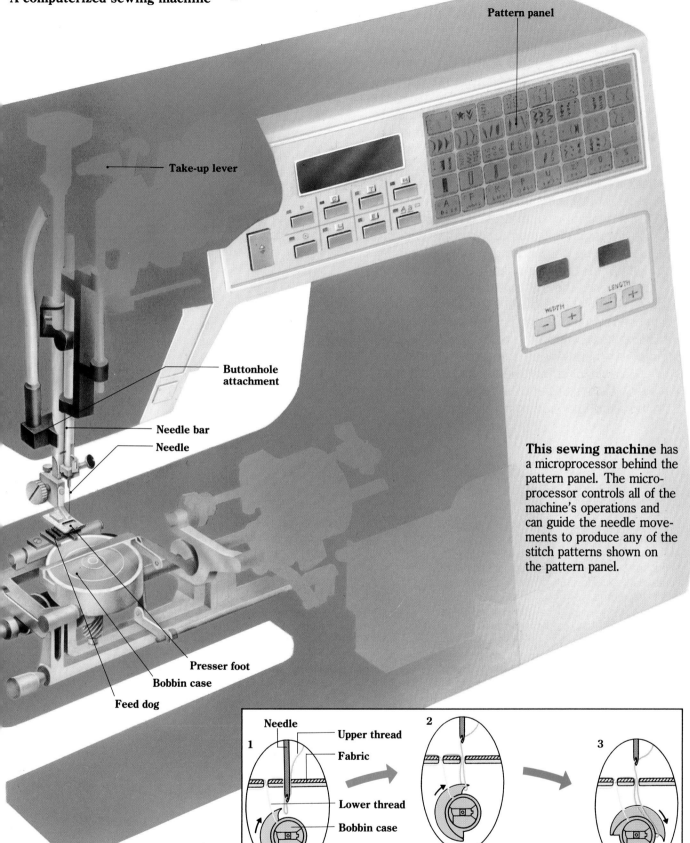

Pattern panel

Take-up lever

WIDTH
LENGTH
— + — +

Buttonhole attachment

Needle bar

Needle

This sewing machine has a microprocessor behind the pattern panel. The microprocessor controls all of the machine's operations and can guide the needle movements to produce any of the stitch patterns shown on the pattern panel.

Presser foot

Bobbin case

Feed dog

Making a basic machine stitch

The needle puts its thread through the fabric, forming a loop (1). The rotating shuttle's hook catches the loop (2) and takes it around the bobbin in the shuttle body (3-4), crossing the needle's thread over the bobbin's (5).

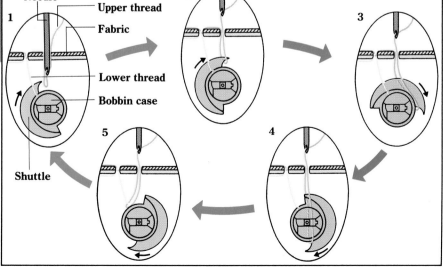

Needle
Upper thread
Fabric
1
2
3
Lower thread
Bobbin case
5
4
Shuttle

How Does a Refrigerator Chill Food?

A refrigerator takes advantage of the way heat moves when a substance undergoes a phase change. When a liquid vaporizes, or evaporates—that is, changes from the liquid phase to the gas phase, as when boiling water changes to steam—it absorbs heat, cooling its surroundings in the process. When the gas condenses, changing back to a liquid, it throws heat off.

A refrigerator circulates a coolant—usually one of a group of chemicals trademarked Freon—through pipes and tubes inside and outside the cooling compartment. Several valves, and a pump called a compressor, control and alter the pressure in the system. The system is designed to put the coolant through two phase changes in two locations. The coolant vaporizes, *absorbing* heat, within the tubes *inside* the cooling compartment. When it enters the tubes *outside* the cooling compartment, the coolant is allowed to condense back into a liquid, so that it *loses* the heat it picked up on the inside.

The refrigeration cycle

The coolant *(below, light blue)* enters the compressor as a gas at low pressure and is subjected to high pressure, which causes it to heat up *(dark red)*. Pumped into the condenser, it turns to liquid and loses heat *(dark blue)*. Capillary tubes take the liquid to the evaporator, where lower pressure lets it become a gas again; during this phase change, it draws heat from the cooling compartment, lowering the temperature.

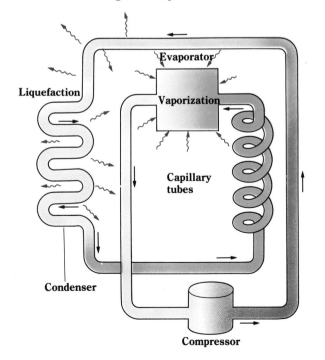

Liquefaction

Evaporator

Vaporization

Capillary tubes

Condenser

Compressor

Inside a refrigerator

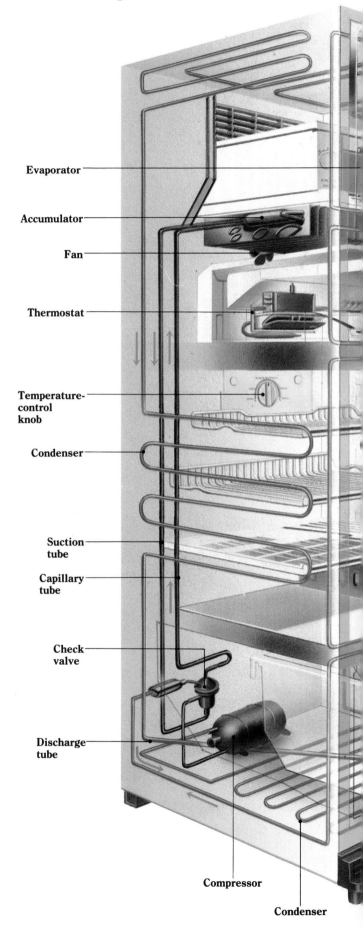

Evaporator

Accumulator

Fan

Thermostat

Temperature-control knob

Condenser

Suction tube

Capillary tube

Check valve

Discharge tube

Compressor

Condenser

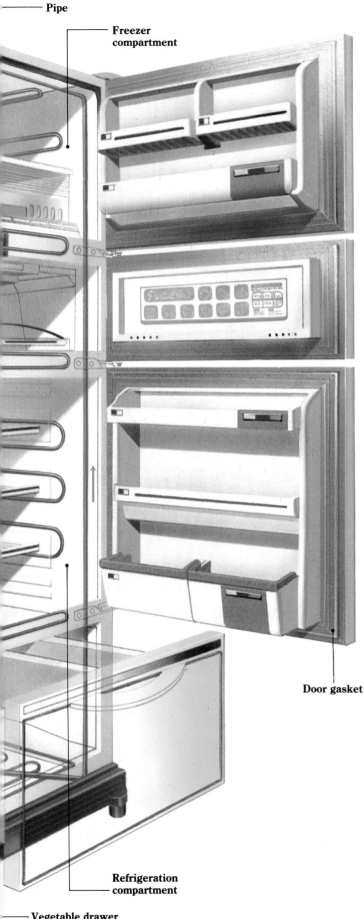

Pipe

Freezer compartment

Door gasket

Refrigeration compartment

Vegetable drawer

Throwing off heat. The refrigerator shown at left has a condenser *(red tubes)* that discharges its heat inside the walls of the cooling and freezing compartments. A more common kind of condenser has coils on the outside of the refrigerator, at the back.

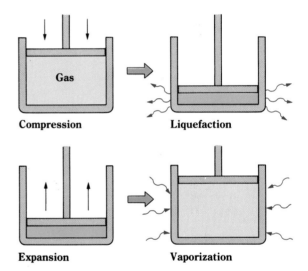

Compression

Liquefaction

Expansion

Vaporization

Pressure and phase changes. A gas under pressure *(top)* turns to liquid and gives off heat. Conversely, when pressure on a confined liquid is reduced *(above),* the liquid vaporizes, drawing heat from its surroundings, thus cooling the area.

How Do Scales Weigh?

A bathroom scale is a spring-balance weighing system. It relies on the principle that a spring expands, or stretches, in proportion to the weight applied to it. When a person steps onto a scale, the platform drops down slightly and the dial turns until the number of pounds the person weighs comes under the indicator needle. Inside the scale, a set of interconnected levers has distributed the weight, dividing the load among four support points, or fulcrums, and pressure points, or springs *(below)*.

As the springs stretch in proportion to the load, they move a notched lever—a rack—in the center of the scale. The rack rotates a pinion gear on the stem of a disk, which is marked in 1-pound gradations around its rim. This dial turns until the needle points to the person's weight. Some newer scales detect the springs' expansion electronically and display the weight digitally—but they are still based on springs.

Inside a bathroom scale

When a person steps on the scale, the weight is distributed evenly to the four corners of the scale by the suspended levers. Force transmitted by the levers stretches the springs.

1 Indicator needle
2 Log-on post
3 Platform
4 Fulcrum
5 Weight lever
6 Rack spring
7 Indicator disk
8 Pinion gear
9 Rack
10 Mainspring
11 Spring tension adjustment

How the levers support weight

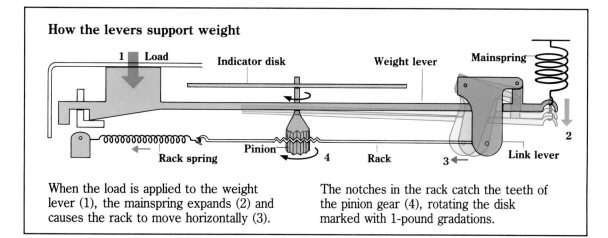

1 Load · Indicator disk · Weight lever · Mainspring · **2** · Rack spring · Pinion · **4** · Rack · **3** · Link lever

When the load is applied to the weight lever (1), the mainspring expands (2) and causes the rack to move horizontally (3).

The notches in the rack catch the teeth of the pinion gear (4), rotating the disk marked with 1-pound gradations.

A spring balance

When a weight is suspended from a spring, the spring stretches until the weight load equals the spring's contraction force—the force with which the spring pulls up. Doubling the weight makes the spring stretch twice as far.

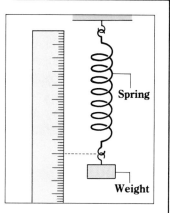

Spring · Weight

The lever-fulcrum-load system

The fraction of the load that bears on the fulcrum *(below)* varies with the position of the load. The nearer the load is to the fulcrum, the smaller the proportion of its weight on the spring.

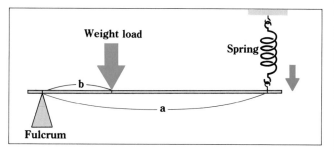

Weight load · Spring · b · a · Fulcrum

How a scale distributes load

When a person steps on the scale's platform, the weight levers underneath distribute the weight load. The weight is carried equally by support points and pressure points.

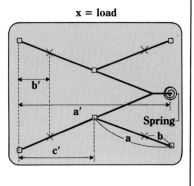

x = load · b′ · a′ · Spring · a · b · c′

What Makes a Water Faucet Work?

Each time someone turns the handle of a water faucet, that person moves a valve and opens or closes a hole at the end of a water pipe. When this hole is opened, a stream of pent-up water is released and gushes out under pressure. Since the pressure behind the water remains constant, the wider the opening is, the more water flows. With a heavy flow, the water pressure is so strong that it would be hard to plug the pipe by hand. But tightening the handle of the faucet closes the opening easily.

The faucet is a combination of simple machines—the wheel and axle, and the screw—that plug the hole with great force while allowing the handle to turn with minimum effort. The handle is a wheel; the stem is an axle with screw threads on it. Turning this threaded axle in its screw-threaded sleeve raises or lowers the entire axle. As the axle is unscrewed to open the faucet, a built-in stopper, called a washer, is lifted out of the way of the water that is pressing on its back. When the valve is reclosed, friction between the threads of the axle and sleeve keeps it closed.

The parts of a water faucet

Handle

Threaded stem

Valve seat

The washer. A movable plug of rubber, fiber, or plastic, the faucet washer is shaped like a doughnut and held in place by a screw.

The washer and its seat

In some faucets the washer fits loosely in the stem *(below, left)* and slides up from water pressure when the handle is turned. In others *(middle and right)*, the washer is attached and is lifted as the handle turns.

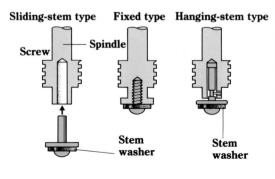

Sliding-stem type   Fixed type   Hanging-stem type

Screw   Spindle

Stem washer   Stem washer

The water system

The water-filtration plant pumps clean water at a constant pressure into the pipes that carry water to household sinks. Turning a faucet handle releases that pressure and lets the water flow.

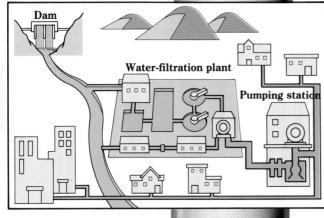

Dam

Water-filtration plant

Pumping station

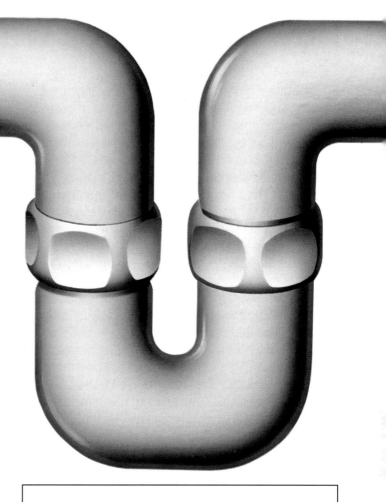

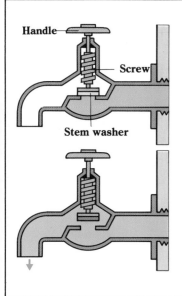

Adjusting the flow

Handle

Screw

Stem washer

When the water faucet is turned off, the water's path is fully closed *(top left)*. The washer seals off the pipe's opening and keeps water from coming out. Turning the handle to open the faucet *(bottom left)* pulls the washer up, allowing water to flow. How far the washer moves depends on how far the handle is turned and how much pressure the water is exerting.

A single-lever faucet

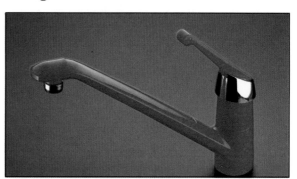

The faucet opens by lifting the lever.

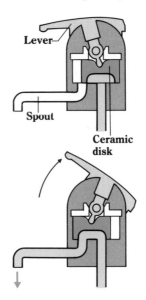

Lever

Spout

Ceramic disk

When the handle is down, as in the type shown here, a ceramic disk *(green)* that serves as a movable valve seat inside the faucet blocks the passage of water *(blue)*. A pin connects this valve seat to the handle, so that lifting the handle slides the valve seat horizontally, moving it partly out of the way. Lifting the handle all the way up *(left, bottom)* opens the water's pathway to its widest.

How Are Clothes Washed by Machine?

An automatic clothes washer is essentially a motorized sink, with an inner washtub perforated with rows of small holes. When dirty clothes and a portion of detergent are put in the inner tub and the machine is started, the washer fills with water and stirs, or agitates, the clothing inside. The back-and-forth motion scrubs the dirt loose in the sudsy water. Then the machine drains the soapy water by spinning the inner tub so that centrifugal force flings the water out of the holes. The machine refills with clean water, agitates the clothes again to rinse away the detergent, and empties the water. Finally the machine spins the inner tub at high speed in order to wring as much water as possible from the clothes.

All of these steps are coordinated by a timer in the machine. Other controls govern the amount and temperature of the water used and how long and how hard the agitators scrub the clothes.

Inside a washing machine

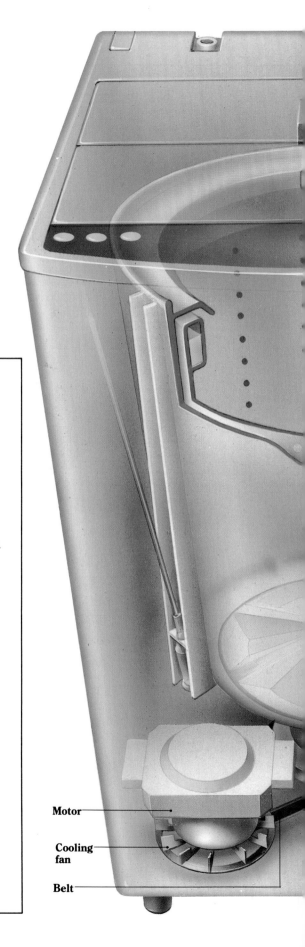

Motor

Cooling fan

Belt

Getting the dirt out

Water and mechanical action together can flush away dirt from fabrics. But some dirt does not dissolve in water, so detergent is added to the water to help remove such soils from fabrics.

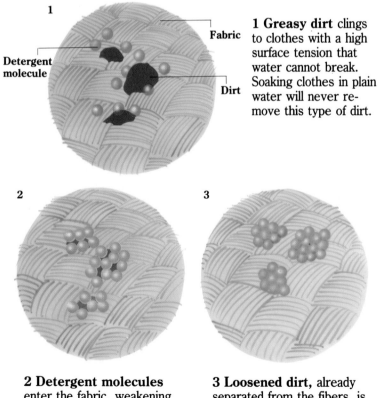

1

Detergent molecule

Fabric

Dirt

1 Greasy dirt clings to clothes with a high surface tension that water cannot break. Soaking clothes in plain water will never remove this type of dirt.

2

3

2 Detergent molecules enter the fabric, weakening and releasing the bonds that hold the dirt to the fibers.

3 Loosened dirt, already separated from the fibers, is flushed away by water with the detergent molecules.

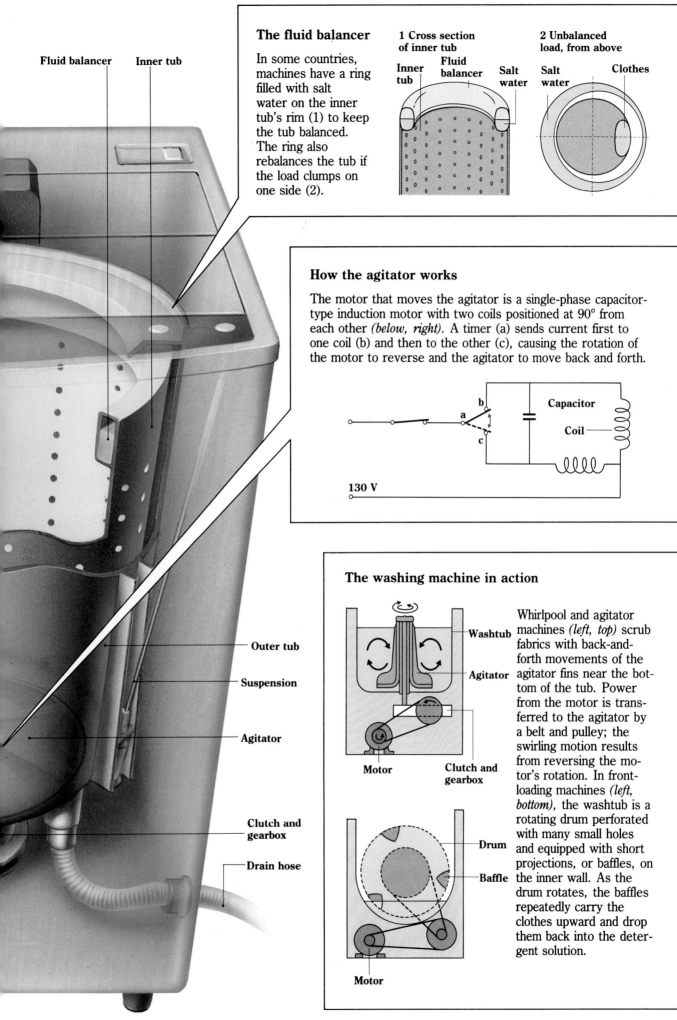

The fluid balancer

In some countries, machines have a ring filled with salt water on the inner tub's rim (1) to keep the tub balanced. The ring also rebalances the tub if the load clumps on one side (2).

1 Cross section of inner tub

Inner tub · Fluid balancer · Salt water

2 Unbalanced load, from above

Salt water · Clothes

How the agitator works

The motor that moves the agitator is a single-phase capacitor-type induction motor with two coils positioned at 90° from each other *(below, right)*. A timer (a) sends current first to one coil (b) and then to the other (c), causing the rotation of the motor to reverse and the agitator to move back and forth.

b · a · c · Capacitor · Coil

130 V

The washing machine in action

Washtub · Agitator · Motor · Clutch and gearbox

Drum · Baffle · Motor

Whirlpool and agitator machines *(left, top)* scrub fabrics with back-and-forth movements of the agitator fins near the bottom of the tub. Power from the motor is transferred to the agitator by a belt and pulley; the swirling motion results from reversing the motor's rotation. In front-loading machines *(left, bottom),* the washtub is a rotating drum perforated with many small holes and equipped with short projections, or baffles, on the inner wall. As the drum rotates, the baffles repeatedly carry the clothes upward and drop them back into the detergent solution.

Fluid balancer · Inner tub

Outer tub

Suspension

Agitator

Clutch and gearbox

Drain hose

What Is a Security System?

A security system consists of electronic sensors connected to a central control, or receiver. The sensors gather information in and around the house and relay it to the receiver. In case of a disruption, the receiver sends alarm signals to a security company. This cutaway view of a house shows five kinds of alarm sensors and how they connect to the receiver. The small illustrations show different kinds of alarm systems, numbered to match the main drawing. Sensors use various means to locate trouble. Some send infrared or high-frequency sound waves to report any kind of interference (3-4); others open or close circuits magnetically (2) or detect vibrations (1), while still others sense infrared heat radiated by moving human bodies (5).

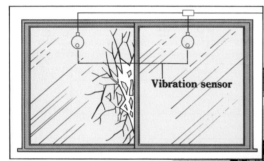

1 Vibrations of breaking glass trip a sensor.

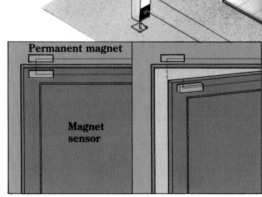

2 Moving a magnet closes the alarm circuit.

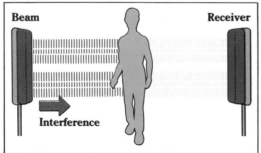

3 A broken infrared beam sets off the alarm.

1 Glass-break sensors react to the vibrations of shattering glass.

2 In a magnetic sensor, a circuit opens or closes, tripping the alarm when the magnet is pulled away from the sensor.

3 A beam-interference alarm sends infrared rays to a beam detector. When an intruder breaks the beam, an alarm sounds.

Home intrusion detectors

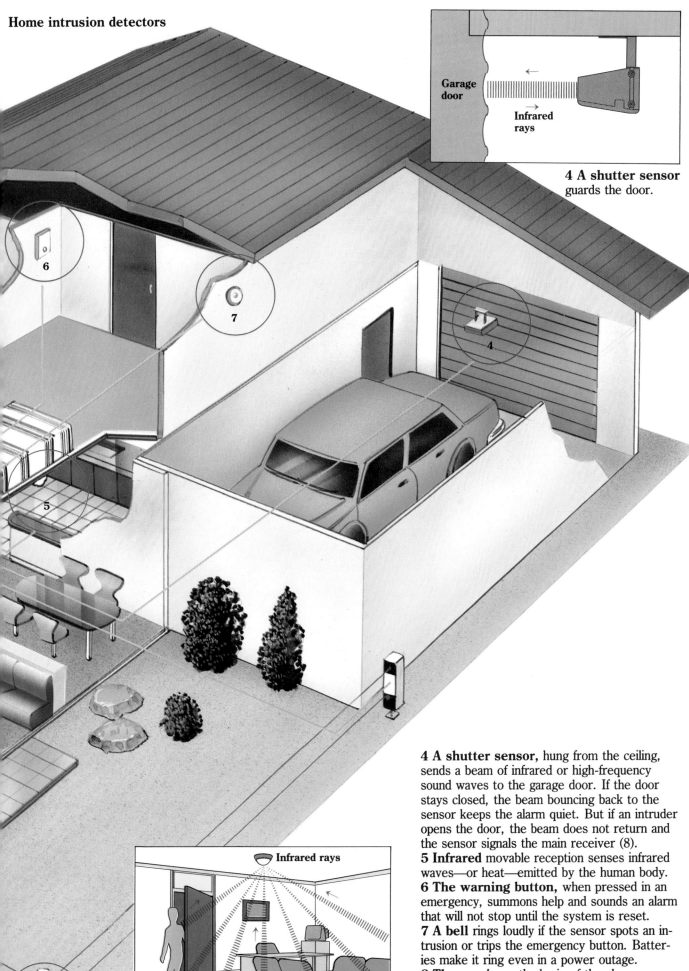

4 A shutter sensor guards the door.

Garage door

Infrared rays

Infrared rays

5 Infrared sensor detects body heat.

4 A shutter sensor, hung from the ceiling, sends a beam of infrared or high-frequency sound waves to the garage door. If the door stays closed, the beam bouncing back to the sensor keeps the alarm quiet. But if an intruder opens the door, the beam does not return and the sensor signals the main receiver (8).

5 Infrared movable reception senses infrared waves—or heat—emitted by the human body.

6 The warning button, when pressed in an emergency, summons help and sounds an alarm that will not stop until the system is reset.

7 A bell rings loudly if the sensor spots an intrusion or trips the emergency button. Batteries make it ring even in a power outage.

8 The receiver, the brain of the alarm system, gets electrical signals from the sensors, sounds a warning, and calls for help.

How Does a Dishwasher Clean Dishes?

Dishwasher at work

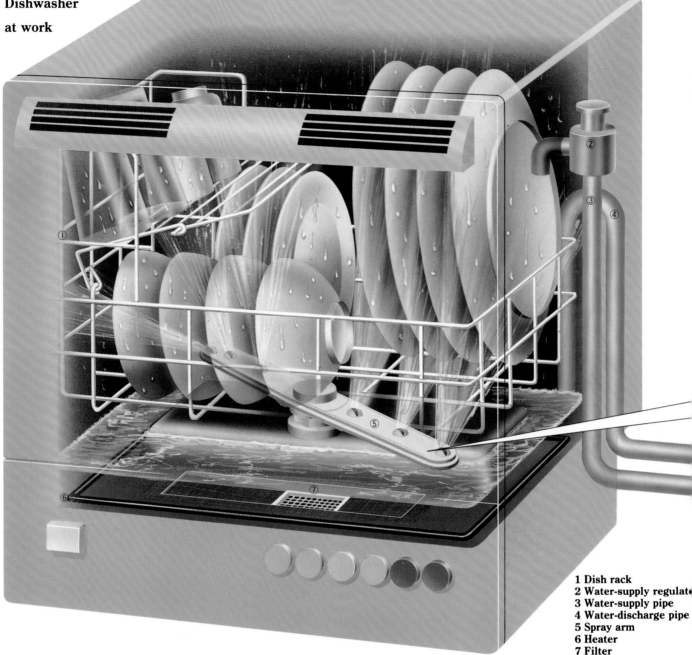

1 Dish rack
2 Water-supply regulat
3 Water-supply pipe
4 Water-discharge pipe
5 Spray arm
6 Heater
7 Filter

The wash-drain-rinse-dry cycles

1 Wash. When the machine starts, water flows into the bottom of the dishwasher. The heating element heats the water, and the machine adds detergent. The wash pump forces the water at high pressure through a pipe and into the spray arm; soapy water shoots out the nozzles and onto the dishes. Then it falls to the bottom and is filtered and sprayed onto the dishes again.
2 Drain. The wash motor turns off.

The dirty water falls to the bottom, and the discharge pump expels it.
3 Rinse. Fresh water is let into the bottom of the dishwasher. The wash pump sprays clean water onto the dishes several times to rinse them.
4 Dry. The fan blows air across the dishes and out a vent, carrying moisture out with it. A heater may switch on intermittently, to speed the evaporation of water from the surface of the dishes.

1 Washing

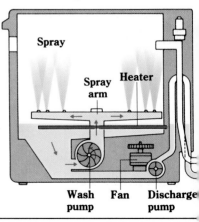

Automatic dishwashers use jets of hot and cold water, with special detergents mixed in, to clean dirty dishes. The dishes must first be arranged in racks so that they are spaced apart. As the machine runs, water jets force hot, soapy water into every corner and onto every dish surface. The water pressure is powerful enough to flush away all kinds of foods. The high-pressure jets also turn the spray arm; by shooting out from the holes in the arm at an angle, the jets cause the arm to rotate in the opposite direction from the spraying water.

In addition, the dishwasher heats the water to about 160° F. At this temperature water is hot enough to scald hands and can liquefy and rinse away fat and grime. Dried-on foods such as eggs and milk are another kind of problem. To handle these stubborn residues, some newer dishwashers have been built to soak dishes *(below)* before beginning the spray-washing cycle.

Rotation of the spray arm

In accord with the law that every action causes an equal and opposite reaction, water shooting from the spray-arm nozzles makes the arm rotate the opposite way.

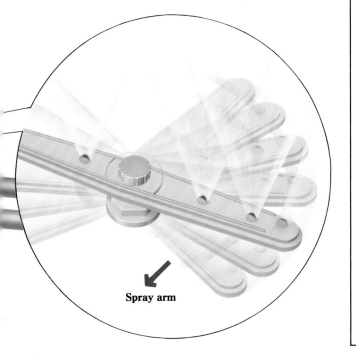

Spray arm

Soaking before spraying

To soften sticky or dried-on foods, some dishwashers fill up with hot or cold water to soak all the dishes before the spray-washing cycle begins.

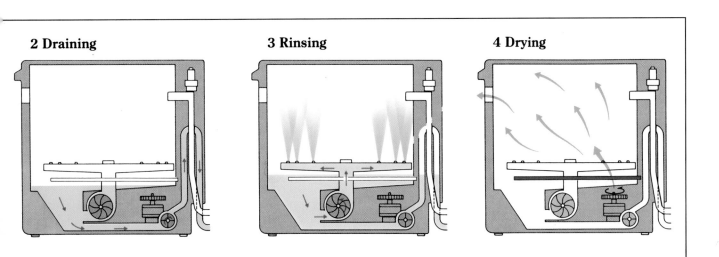

2 Draining

3 Rinsing

4 Drying

How Do Electric Power Meters Work?

To know how much to charge each household for the electricity it uses, the power company installs a meter that measures the current flowing into that house. The unit of measurement is the kilowatt-hour—an hour's supply of electrical energy at a power of 1,000 watts.

The power meter makes use of the fact, discovered in the early nineteenth century by several European scientists, that a coil of wire carrying an electric current exerts a force on a permanent magnet. In an electric power meter, this force moves a spinning disk. A permanent magnet provides a braking effect, keeping the disk's movement proportional to the strength of the current. The disk is linked by gears to a counter *(below, right)* that records the number of rotations of the disk. These rotations depend on, and thus measure, the amount of power used.

Circuitry of the power meter

The meter works like an electric motor to turn an aluminum disk. As the disk rotates, it turns the dials of a counter, which record the amount of electricity used in the house.

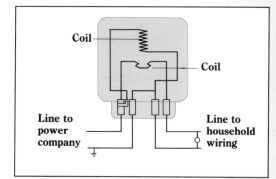

A household power meter and its circuit.

A disk turned by magnetism

In 1824, François Arago discovered that if a copper disk is placed between—but not touching—the poles of a permanent magnet *(top right)* and the magnet is turned *(bottom right)*, the disk rotates to follow the magnet. Moving the magnet changes the magnetic field around the disk and retards the pull of the magnet. The disk rotates like a motor but always lags slightly behind the motion of the magnet.

Cutaway of a power meter

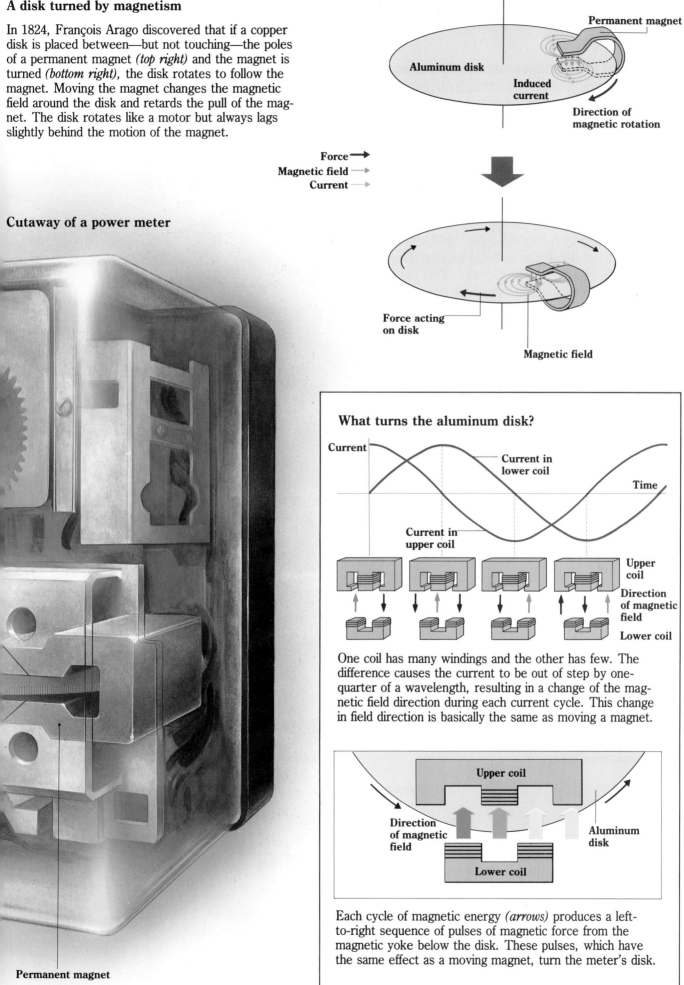

Aluminum disk

Permanent magnet

Induced current

Direction of magnetic rotation

Force ➡
Magnetic field ➡
Current ➡

Force acting on disk

Magnetic field

Permanent magnet

What turns the aluminum disk?

Current

Current in lower coil

Time

Current in upper coil

Upper coil

Direction of magnetic field

Lower coil

One coil has many windings and the other has few. The difference causes the current to be out of step by one-quarter of a wavelength, resulting in a change of the magnetic field direction during each current cycle. This change in field direction is basically the same as moving a magnet.

Upper coil

Direction of magnetic field

Aluminum disk

Lower coil

Each cycle of magnetic energy *(arrows)* produces a left-to-right sequence of pulses of magnetic force from the magnetic yoke below the disk. These pulses, which have the same effect as a moving magnet, turn the meter's disk.

What Turns Thermostats On and Off?

Thermostats, or temperature-control devices, regulate irons, heaters, ovens, refrigerators, and air conditioners. Each kind of thermostat takes advantage of the physical properties of its materials. The metals in a thermistor, or thermal resistor, for example, lose their resistance to electricity as they heat up. Semiconductor sensors work similarly, providing a good pathway for current or a poor one, depending on temperature. By contrast, in a gas-pressure sensor, often used in refrigerators, the gas expands when warming up and inflates a bellows that trips a switch to begin the cooling cycle. The electric iron shown below uses the most common type of thermostat—a bimetal thermal sensor.

An iron with a thermostat

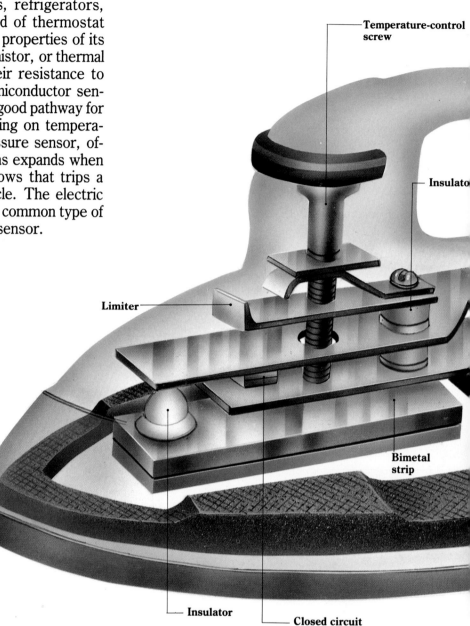

Temperature-control screw

Insulator

Limiter

Bimetal strip

Insulator

Closed circuit

Temperature control

A thermistor is a heat-sensitive electrical switch: Heat decreases its electrical resistance *(right)*, letting current flow. A gas-pressure sensor *(far right)* works in a refrigerator's evaporator. As the temperature rises, the gas expands, activating a bellows and closing a circuit that turns on the compressor. As the temperature falls, the gas contracts, breaking the circuit and turning the compressor off.

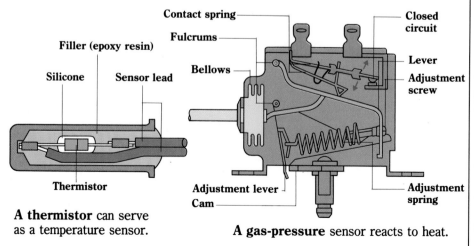

Filler (epoxy resin)

Silicone

Sensor lead

Thermistor

A thermistor can serve as a temperature sensor.

Contact spring

Fulcrums

Bellows

Closed circuit

Lever

Adjustment screw

Adjustment lever

Cam

Adjustment spring

A gas-pressure sensor reacts to heat.

A bimetal strip is the temperature control in an iron. It is made of a layer of ferronickel alloy, which expands little, welded to a layer of brass, which expands more at the same temperature, breaking the circuit.

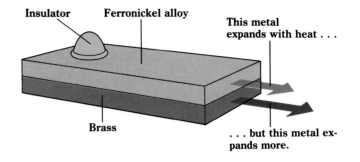

Insulator Ferronickel alloy

This metal expands with heat . . .

Brass

. . . but this metal expands more.

How the sensor regulates heat

The metals in a bimetal thermostat *(below)* expand at different rates when heated. The metal in the top layer expands less. When the iron is on, high heat warps the lower strip, opening the circuit to stop the current. As the iron cools, the strip flattens, the circuit closes, and current flows again.

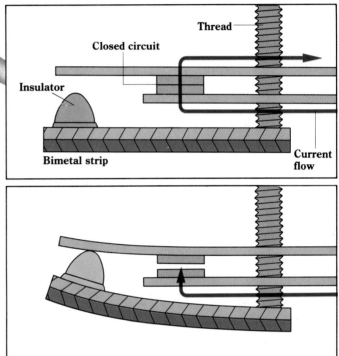

Thread

Closed circuit

Insulator

Bimetal strip

Current flow

The circuit closes *(top)* and opens *(bottom)* using a bimetal heat sensor.

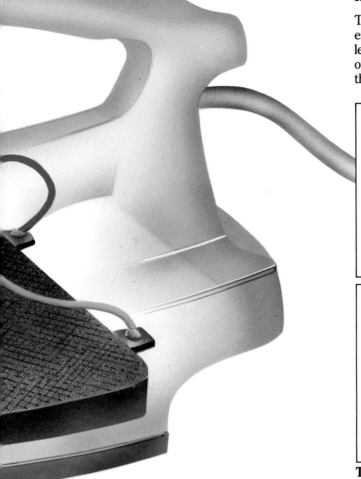

Heating element

Light   Resistor   AC

Thermostat

Heat control in an iron. When the thermal sensor closes the circuit, current warms the heating element and lights the lamp to indicate that the iron is heating.

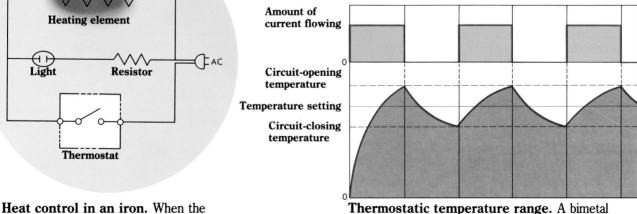

Amount of current flowing

Circuit-opening temperature

Temperature setting

Circuit-closing temperature

Thermostatic temperature range. A bimetal thermostat closes a circuit at one temperature and opens it at another.

How Does an Air Conditioner Cool?

An air conditioner works much like a refrigerator: It absorbs heat in one place and disperses it in another. Both appliances contain pipes and tubes in which they circulate a coolant fluid, usually one of a family of chemicals called Freon. Both put the fluid through phase changes—evaporation and condensation—causing it to gain heat and then lose it.

In a window-mounted air conditioner *(right)*, the evaporator—the chilling part of the unit—faces into the room. As the coolant inside the evaporator's coils changes from a liquid to a gas, it draws heat from its surroundings. The evaporator fan blows warm air from the room across the cold evaporator coils, cooling the air and returning it *(blue arrow)* to the room. A divider inside the air conditioner keeps hot, outside air from entering through the window.

The coolant, now a gas, is pumped to the compressor, which subjects it to high pressure—heating the gas in the process—and forces it through the capillary tubes and into the condenser. There the pressure is lower, and the gas undergoes the opposite phase change: It turns to a liquid, losing heat along the way. The condenser faces the outdoors, and the condenser fan blows outdoor air across the condenser coils; the heat *(red arrow)* is dispersed to the outdoors.

A window air conditioner

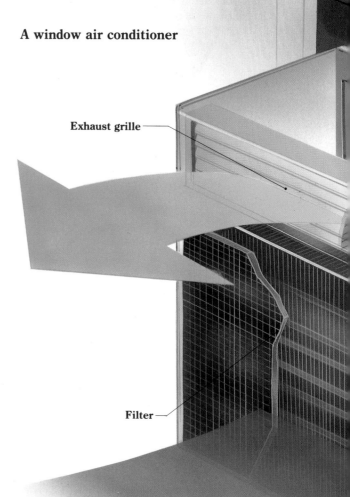

Exhaust grille

Filter

The reversible heat pump

A special type of air conditioner, called a heat pump, can reverse the flow of coolant—and with it the direction of the heat exchange—so that the unit heats the room instead of cooling it. When the unit is used to cool indoor air *(right, top),* cooling occurs on the indoor side of the unit, where the coolant is evaporated *(blue coils),* and the heat is discharged outdoors, where the coolant is condensed *(pink coils).*

But in this reversible system, resetting a four-way valve *(red)* reverses the coolant flow. The indoor coils, which had served as the evaporator, then become the condenser *(pink coils)* and discharge heat into the room. The outdoor unit becomes the evaporator *(blue coils),* where the coolant absorbs the heat that it will carry indoors.

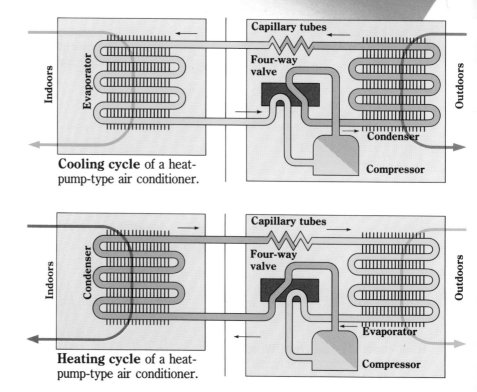

Cooling cycle of a heat-pump-type air conditioner.

Heating cycle of a heat-pump-type air conditioner.

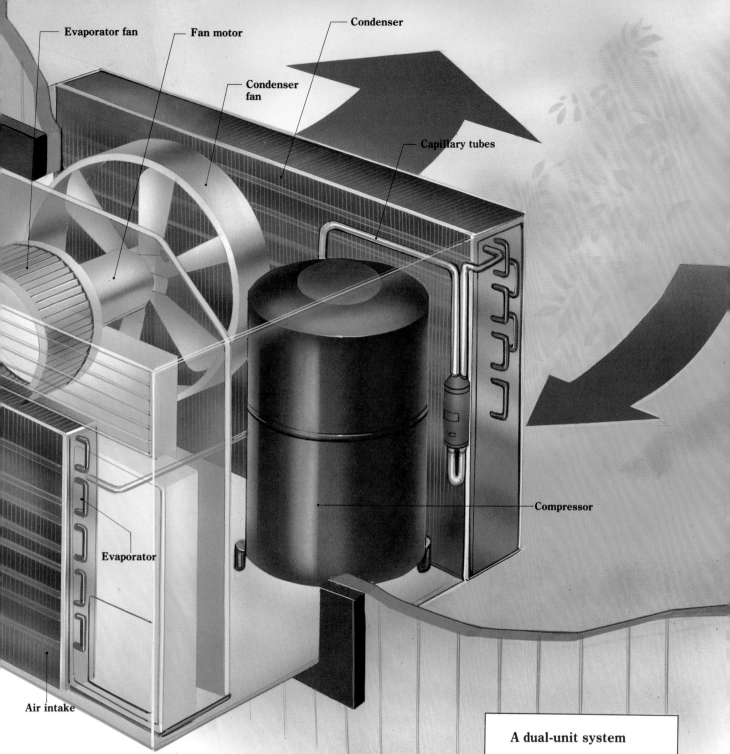

Evaporator fan — Fan motor

Condenser

Condenser fan

Capillary tubes

Compressor

Evaporator

Air intake

The compression principle

The two phase changes in a cooling cycle are not equal in their energy requirements. The coolant evaporates of its own accord, because pressure on it is released. But changing the gas back to a liquid takes energy. An air conditioner uses electricity to run the compressor, which pumps the gas into a smaller space, putting it under greater pressure. A rotary compressor—compact, efficient, and quiet—has an off-center rotor *(right)* for a piston. In one rotation *(right, 1–4)*, the rotor simultaneously draws in more gas *(blue)* and pushes the previously admitted gas *(purple)* into the capillary tubes.

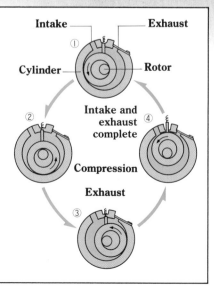

Intake — Exhaust

Cylinder — Rotor

①

Intake and exhaust complete

② ④

Compression

Exhaust

③

A dual-unit system

Dual units split the parts of an air conditioner. Only the evaporator is inside; the compressor and condenser are outside. Coolant circulates throughout.

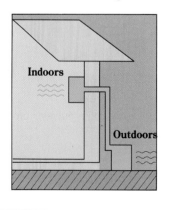

Indoors

Outdoors

What Is a Dehumidifier?

Built of components similar to an air conditioner's, a dehumidifier condenses water vapor out of a room's air by blowing the air across a set of cold coils. As in an air conditioner, the dehumidifier's coils are cold because evaporation is going on inside them. And the rest of the cycle involves compression and condensation, to restore the circulating coolant to its liquid phase.

A dehumidifier, however, is designed not to cool a room but to leave its temperature the same. To retain the same temperature, the machine blows the cooled-and-dried air over its condenser coils, reheating the air *(below)* before returning it to the room. Even at such summery temperatures as 85° F., lower humidity makes people more comfortable, because it lets moisture evaporate from the skin.

A dehumidifier in action

As humid air flows over the dehumidifier's cold evaporator coils, water vapor carried in the air condenses onto the coils. From there the water drips into a collector tank *(below, bottom)*, to be emptied or drained away. A humidity sensor keeps the dehumidifier running whenever the relative humidity in the room is above 60 percent. A dehumidifier designed for one room can remove about a gallon of water a day from the air.

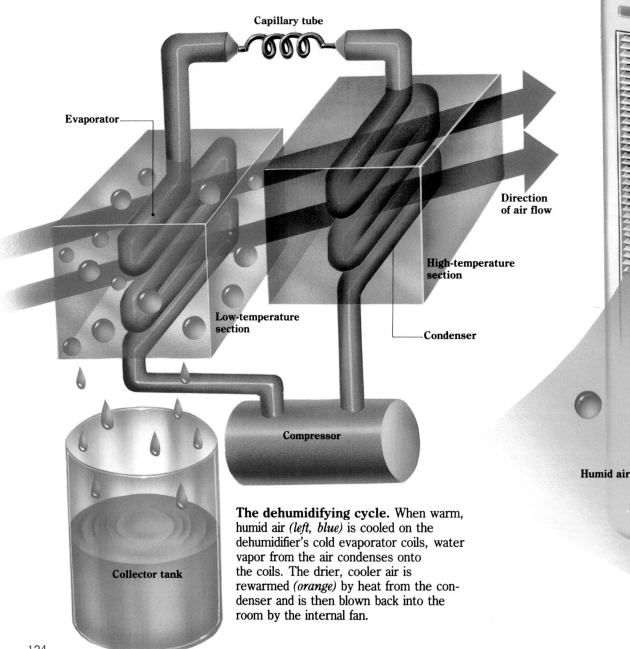

Capillary tube

Evaporator

Low-temperature section

Filter

Direction of air flow

High-temperature section

Condenser

Compressor

Collector tank

Humid air

The dehumidifying cycle. When warm, humid air *(left, blue)* is cooled on the dehumidifier's cold evaporator coils, water vapor from the air condenses onto the coils. The drier, cooler air is rewarmed *(orange)* by heat from the condenser and is then blown back into the room by the internal fan.

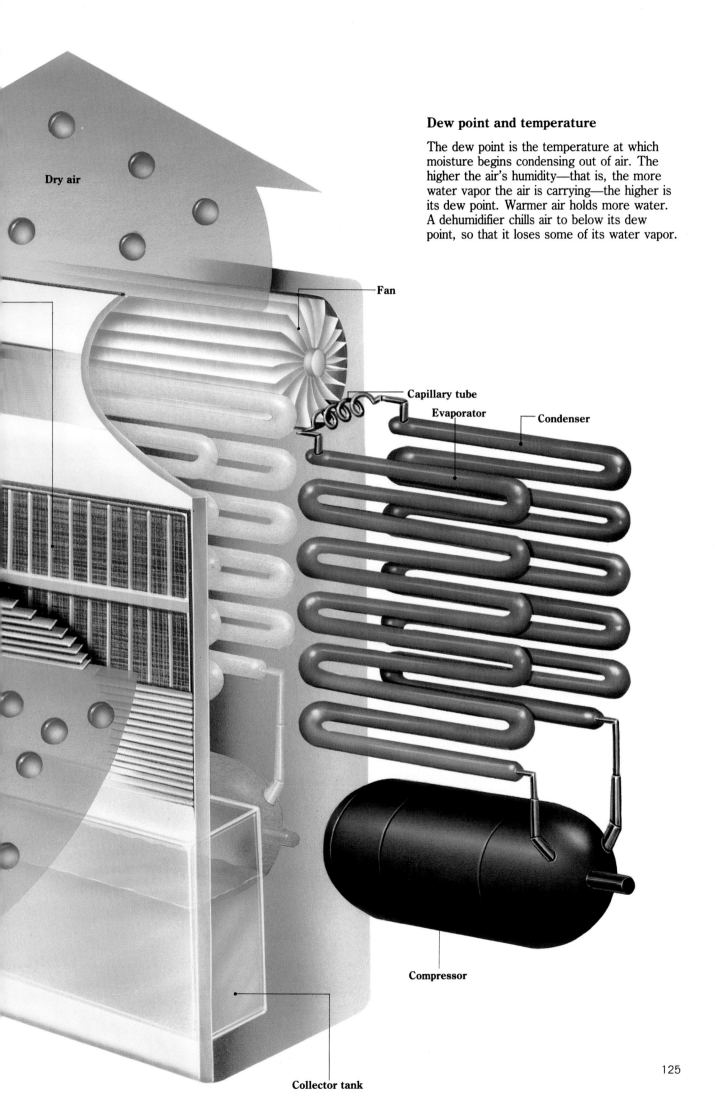

Dry air

Fan

Capillary tube

Evaporator

Condenser

Dew point and temperature

The dew point is the temperature at which moisture begins condensing out of air. The higher the air's humidity—that is, the more water vapor the air is carrying—the higher is its dew point. Warmer air holds more water. A dehumidifier chills air to below its dew point, so that it loses some of its water vapor.

Compressor

Collector tank

125

6
Medical Marvels

In the last 100 years or so, scientists and engineers have developed a wondrous array of instruments and machinery that prevent, diagnose, or treat illness and trauma. The most familiar of these monitor vital signs such as temperature, blood pressure, and heart rate. Electronic thermometers, for example, are able to calculate body temperature in 30 seconds or less, while electrocardiographs translate the complex rhythms of the heart into wave patterns that can be read by specialists.

Other instruments open windows on the body's inner landscape. A CAT (computerized axial tomography) scanner, for instance, produces three-dimensional x-rays of any body part in seconds. And a fiberscope—a slender probe with a tiny camera at its tip—delivers video images of the internal workings of the stomach, pancreas, and other organs in real time.

The boldest medical innovations may be those that function in the absence or failure of a major organ, such as the mechanical heart and the pacemaker. These and other pioneering devices, explained in the pages that follow, offer humans unprecedented hope for longer and healthier lives.

Medical machines use the latest electronic, nuclear, and optical technologies to aid health workers in promoting wellness, diagnosing and fighting disease, and overcoming physical defects.

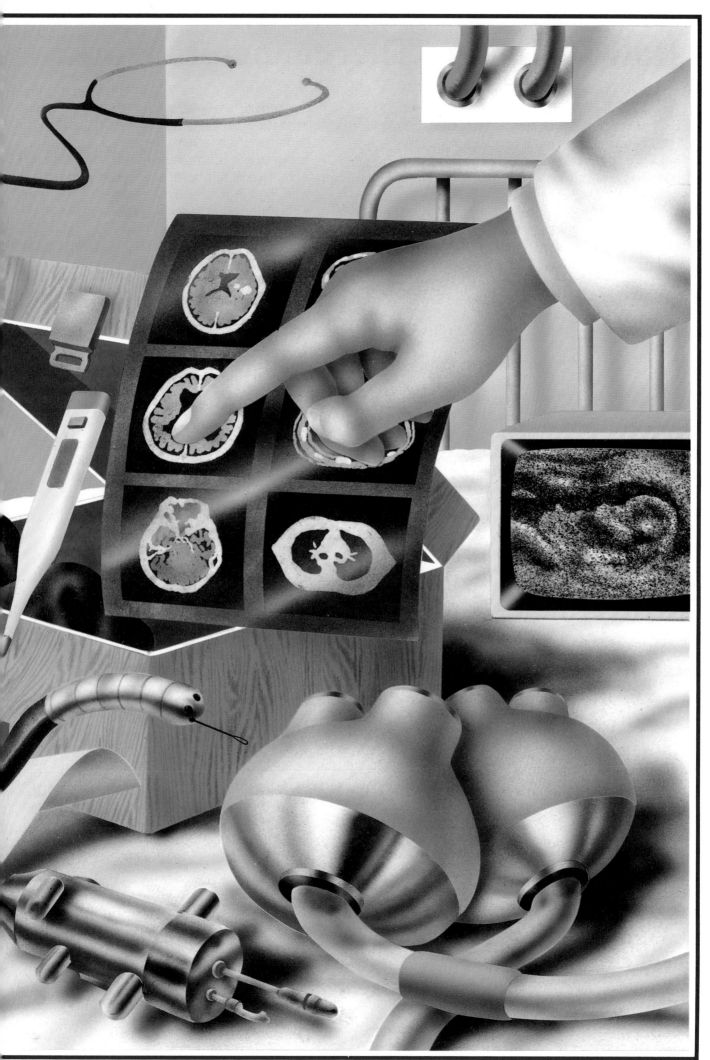

How Do Instant Thermometers Work?

An old-fashioned glass thermometer must be held under the arm or tongue for 3 or more minutes before it delivers a final reading, called an equilibrium reading. An electronic thermometer, however, can give an equilibrium reading in 30 seconds or less.

Embedded in the tip of the electronic thermometer is a tiny thermistor, a heat-sensitive device that registers temperature changes as electrical fluctuations. These fluxes are sent to a computerized sensor, which converts them into temperature readings and channels them to the thermometer's microprocessor.

Inside the microprocessor, the readings are matched to a temperature-progression curve stored in the processor's memory. From this, the thermometer quickly estimates what the equilibrium temperature will be. Although such a reading is only a prediction, it accurately indicates whether a fever is slight or severe.

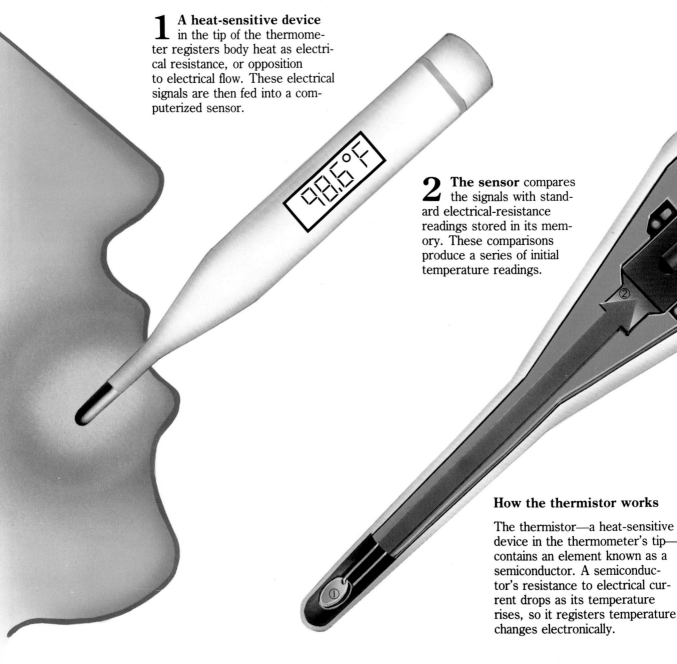

1 **A heat-sensitive device** in the tip of the thermometer registers body heat as electrical resistance, or opposition to electrical flow. These electrical signals are then fed into a computerized sensor.

2 **The sensor** compares the signals with standard electrical-resistance readings stored in its memory. These comparisons produce a series of initial temperature readings.

How the thermistor works

The thermistor—a heat-sensitive device in the thermometer's tip—contains an element known as a semiconductor. A semiconductor's resistance to electrical current drops as its temperature rises, so it registers temperature changes electronically.

Wonderworks revealed

An electronic thermometer contains six main parts, numbered on the illustration below: a heat-sensitive thermistor (1), a computerized sensor (2), a microprocessor (3), a numerical display window (4), an internal switch (5), and a battery (6). The workings of each part are described on these pages.

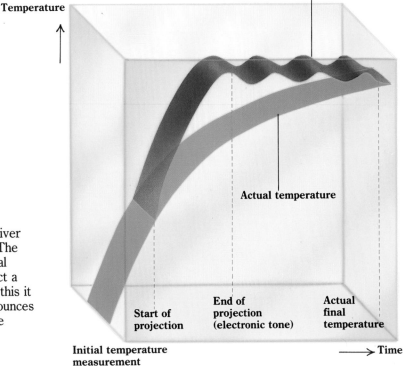

98.6°F

The thermometer's energy saver

An internal switch prolongs the life of the thermometer's power source by automatically turning off the power whenever the thermometer is returned to its case or whenever it is not used for a certain time period. Thanks to this energy-saving feature, the thermometer's tiny battery can provide years of service.

4 **The final temperature** prediction appears as numerals in a liquid-crystal display window. In some electronic thermometers, the readout remains illuminated until the thermometer is reset.

3 **A microprocessor** attached to the sensor plugs the temperature readings into a complex mathematical formula. The result is a prediction of what the final temperature reading will be, based on the rate at which the initial readings increased during a given time period.

Predicting temperature

The electronic thermometer uses a shortcut to deliver its temperature readings in less than 30 seconds. The thermometer's microprocessor applies mathematical equations to a set of initial measurements to project a temperature-rise curve (*right, purple band*). From this it predicts the equilibrium temperature, which it announces with an electronic tone. The projected temperature tends to be slightly higher than the actual value.

Temperature

Projected temperature

Actual temperature

Start of projection

End of projection (electronic tone)

Actual final temperature

Initial temperature measurement

Time

How Is Blood Pressure Taken?

The heart is a living pump that delivers blood to all parts of the body. The force with which the blood moves through the arteries is known as blood pressure. Maximum blood pressure, called systolic pressure, coincides with the rhythmic contractions of the heart that drive blood into the arteries. Minimum, or diastolic, blood pressure occurs between heartbeats, when the heart expands to fill itself with a fresh supply of blood.

Using a device known as a sphygmomanometer, medical personnel can measure both phases of a person's blood pressure, as shown below.

Stanching the flow

To measure blood pressure, a nurse or doctor pumps air into an inflatable cuff wrapped around the arm *(below)*. This temporarily stops the flow of blood to the lower arm. When the mercury gauge registers 150 to 200 milligrams of pressure *(right)*, the air is slowly released.

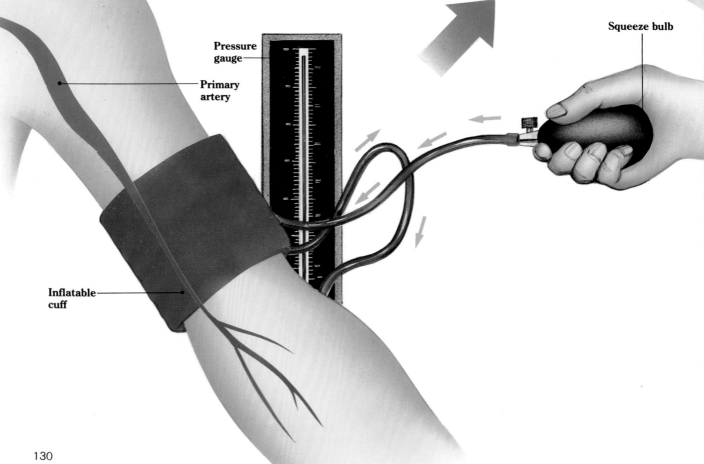

Stethoscope

Pressure gauge

Primary artery

Squeeze bulb

Inflatable cuff

Gauging systolic pressure

As the pressure in the cuff goes down, a stethoscope is held over the artery. When the cuff pressure decreases to the level of arterial pressure, the tapping of pulsing blood can be heard through the stethoscope. At that instant, the gauge shows the maximum, or systolic, blood pressure.

Measuring diastolic pressure

Further deflating the cuff permits more blood to flow, amplifying the tapping sound to a loud knocking. Then, as the pressure inside the artery subsides between heartbeats, the sound quiets to a murmur. The pressure-gauge reading at which the sound disappears is known as the minimum, or diastolic, blood pressure.

Artery wall

Blood

The sound in the stethoscope

Korotkoff sounds—the slight rapping first heard as the blood-pressure cuff is deflated—are made by the rhythmic pulsating of the walls of an artery, shown in a magnified cross section above. These arterial pulsations send blood from the heart to the limbs.

New and improved

An electronic blood-pressure gauge *(right)* houses built-in microphones, which pick up Korotkoff sounds before they can be detected by the human ear. Tiny motors regulate air pressure in the cuff, making the gauge easy to use.

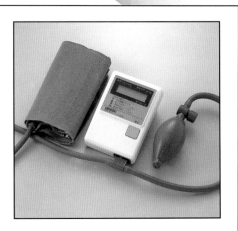

What Is a Mechanical Heart?

On December 2, 1982, surgeon William DeVries performed the first successful implantation of a mechanical heart in a human. The aluminum-and-plastic heart, named Jarvik-7 after the physician who invented it, comprised two pumping chambers, or ventricles, that attached to the upper chambers of the natural heart. The ventricles were in turn linked to an external drive, which used compressed air to regulate the movement of the ventricles' rubber diaphragms. The resulting pulselike rhythm circulated the blood.

Unwieldy and inorganic, a mechanical heart is no match for the real thing. But in the case described above, it prolonged the life of the patient—dentist Barney Frank—for 112 days.

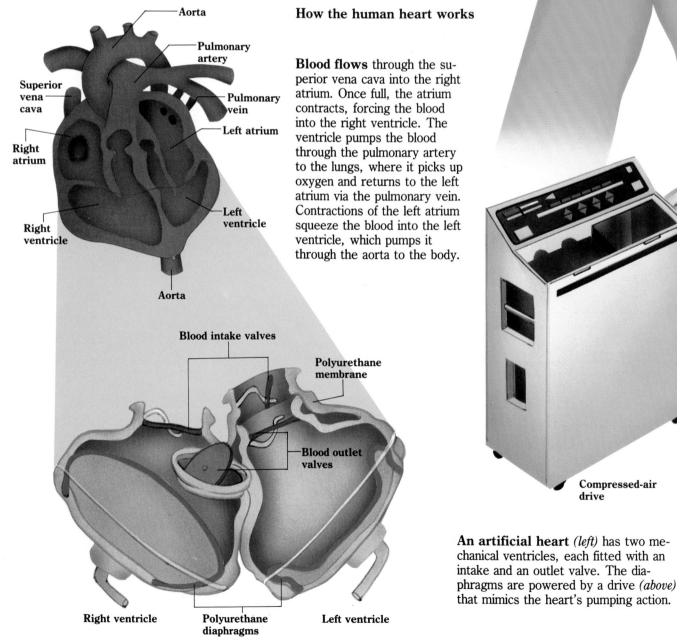

Aorta

Pulmonary artery

Superior vena cava

Pulmonary vein

Left atrium

Right atrium

Left ventricle

Right ventricle

Aorta

Blood intake valves

Polyurethane membrane

Blood outlet valves

Right ventricle

Polyurethane diaphragms

Left ventricle

How the human heart works

Blood flows through the superior vena cava into the right atrium. Once full, the atrium contracts, forcing the blood into the right ventricle. The ventricle pumps the blood through the pulmonary artery to the lungs, where it picks up oxygen and returns to the left atrium via the pulmonary vein. Contractions of the left atrium squeeze the blood into the left ventricle, which pumps it through the aorta to the body.

Compressed-air drive

An artificial heart *(left)* has two mechanical ventricles, each fitted with an intake and an outlet valve. The diaphragms are powered by a drive *(above)* that mimics the heart's pumping action.

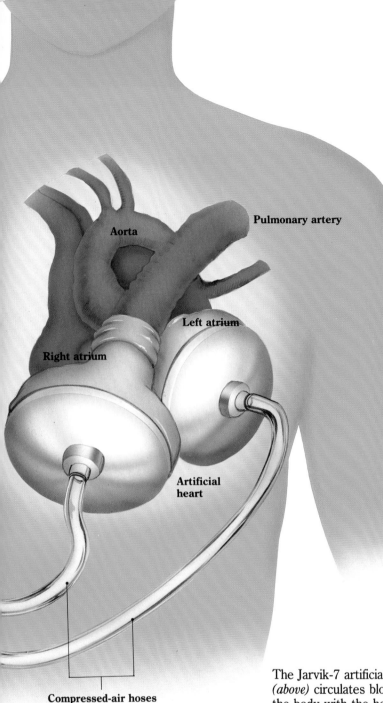

Aorta

Pulmonary artery

Left atrium

Right atrium

Artificial
heart

Compressed-air hoses

Creating an artificial pulse

As shown below, an artificial heart simulates both the resting phase (also called the diastole) and the pumping phase, or systole, of the heart's natural rhythm. During the diastole *(top)*, an external drive creates suction that pulls the diaphragm down, causing blood to fill the ventricle. Then, during the systole, compressed air forces the diaphragm upward *(bottom)*, pumping the blood out.

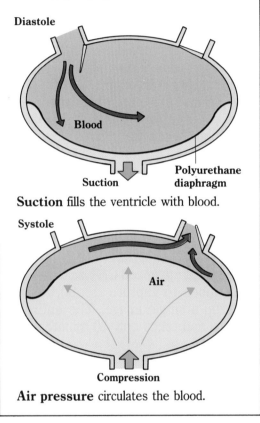

Diastole

Blood

Suction

Polyurethane diaphragm

Suction fills the ventricle with blood.

Systole

Air

Compression

Air pressure circulates the blood.

The Jarvik-7 artificial heart *(above)* circulates blood through the body with the help of an external compressed-air drive. Air hoses attach the compressor to the heart's artificial ventricles via the chest wall.

Heart helpmates

Heart ailments can be remedied by one of the two devices at right, which temporarily take over all or part of the heart's functions. An auxiliary mechanical heart *(right)* pumps blood for short periods while the weakened heart recovers. A pacemaker *(far right)* supplies electrical pulses to regulate the heartbeat.

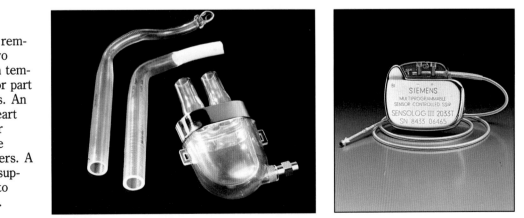

How Do CAT Scanners Work?

Because x-rays can penetrate the human body, they are an ideal tool for diagnosing skeletal ailments, such as bone fractures. Internal organs, however, appear only as vague shadows when x-rayed. To get a clear view of these "shadowy" substances—notably muscle, brain matter, and organ tissues—doctors often turn to a computerized axial tomographic scanner, or CAT scanner. The scanner uses photon detectors and a computer to produce cross-sectional images, or tomograms, of the body's interior.

To obtain a tomogram, technicians place the patient on a table that moves slowly through the CAT scanner. Rotating tubes then beam x-rays at the patient, generating data about successive "slices" of the body as it passes by. Detectors opposite each x-ray tube collect the data and digitize it, or convert it into computer-readable form. From these digitized signals, a computer assembles a tomogram.

The most advanced CAT scanners employ 300 x-ray tubes to capture the 90,000 x-rays that make up a single image. The entire process is painless and takes only 20 minutes to an hour.

A CAT scanner at work

The technology behind the image

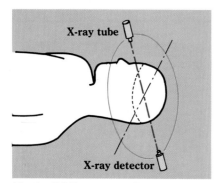

Early CAT scanners featured only one x-ray detector and one x-ray tube. As the two devices rotated in synchronization, the detector collected the x-ray data from the tube.

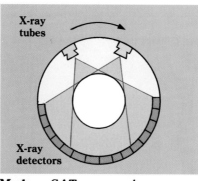

Modern CAT scanners have many tubes and detectors. The tubes emit fan-shaped x-rays, enabling the detectors to collect vast amounts of data. The images are made in seconds.

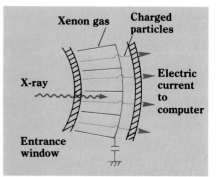

Some detectors contain xenon gas. As the x-rays hit the gas, they create charged particles; these generate an electric current, which the computer converts into an image.

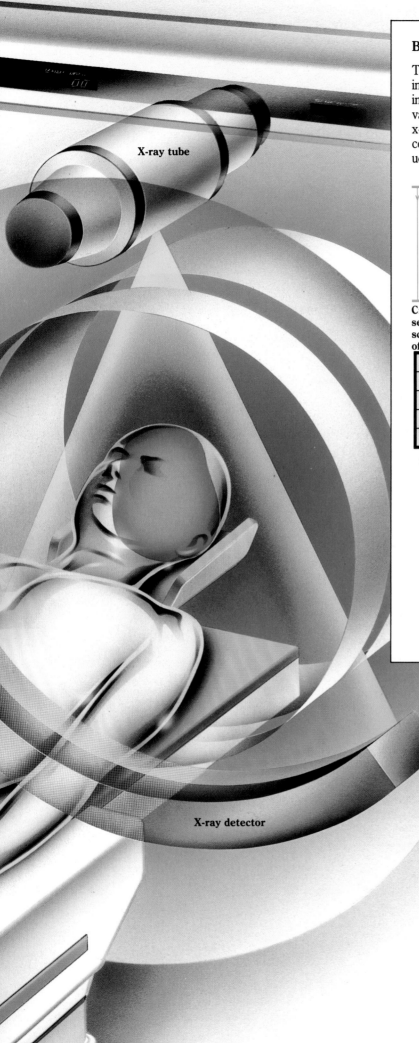

X-ray tube

X-ray detector

Building a tomogram

To turn x-ray data into a cross-sectional image, the computer first divides the area into blocks. It then assigns each block a value, depending on the intensity of the x-rays reaching that block. Finally, it uses complex equations to transform these values into the elements of the image.

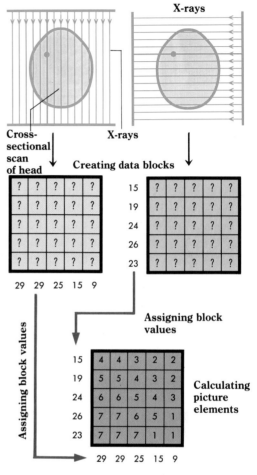

X-rays

X-rays

Cross-sectional scan of head

Creating data blocks

Assigning block values

Assigning block values

Calculating picture elements

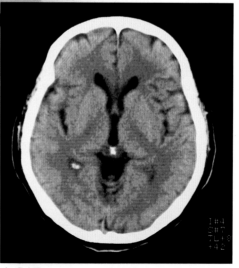

A CAT scanner made this tomogram, showing a human brain in cross section.

What Is an EKG?

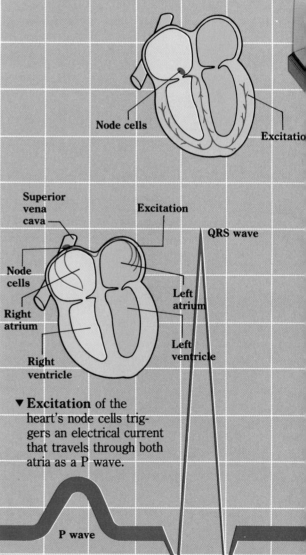

Electrodes

The human heart is powered by electricity. Before each heartbeat, cells called nodes generate a tiny electrical impulse that sets charged particles flowing along the muscle fibers of the heart. This electrical impulse then sparks the chain of rhythmic contractions that make up a single heartbeat.

As the impulse passes through the heart, its speed and intensity fluctuate in a regular pattern. Some of the impulses migrate to the body's surface, where they can be monitored by a device called an electrocardiograph.

Electrodes leading from the electrocardiograph are attached to the patient's chest with a special jelly *(above)*. The electrodes detect the heart's current fluctuations and channel them to the electrocardiograph *(far right)*, which records the changes as wave-forms on a moving scroll of paper. This record is known as an electrocardiogram, or EKG. If the patient's heart is healthy, the EKG takes the form of a repeating series of wave-forms. Deviations from the pattern betray a possible heart condition.

This electrocardiogram reveals the wave patterns generated by a healthy heart. P waves, QRS waves, and T waves all recur in a rhythmic sequence.

What the squiggles mean

Node cells

Excitatio

Superior vena cava

Excitation

QRS wave

Node cells

Left atrium

Right atrium

Left ventricle

Right ventricle

▼ **Excitation** of the heart's node cells triggers an electrical current that travels through both atria as a P wave.

P wave

▲ **As the heart** contracts, a high-speed wave train echoes through the ventricles. It appears on the EKG as a spike, or QRS complex.

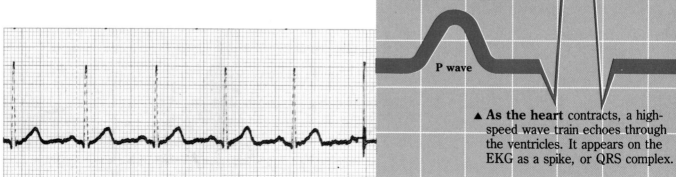

Exciting the heart to action

A change in the electrical charge of the heart's muscle cells stimulates the heart rhythm and its characteristic signature of EKG waves. At rest *(below, left)*, the cell membranes carry a positive charge because the surrounding fluid contains positively charged particles, or ions.

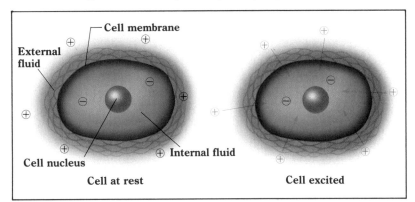

Cell at rest   Cell excited

Just before each heartbeat, a minute electrical jolt causes the ions to pass through the cell membranes *(above, right)*. The membranes become negatively charged and excite a new heart cycle.

Amplifier

Magnet

Recording pen

From heart to chart

Electrodes attached to the patient's chest feed current fluxes from the heart to an amplifier in the EKG. The amplified signals are then shunted to a coil inside a magnet; here they interact with the magnetic field, creating a force that moves the recording pen.

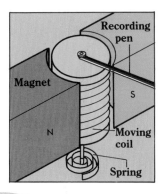

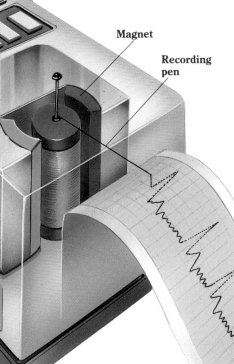

T wave

▲ **When the heart** relaxes, ready for the next wave cycle, mild T waves wash over the ventricles.

Can a Fiberscope See inside the Body?

A fiberscope is a slender, snakelike viewing instrument that allows doctors to see inside the organs of the human body. Early models, known as endoscopes, were rigid tubes with an eyepiece at one end and a viewing lens and light source at the other.

Although engineers gradually improved the flexibility of the endoscope, the instrument's viewing power remained poor until the advent of fiber optics—the technology that transfers light and pictures along hairlike fibers of glass or plastic. In a modern fiberscope, thousands of these filaments are bound together in a thin, supple cable. Light from a lamp or laser at the probe end of the instrument travels through these fibers to a tiny photographic or video camera at the viewing end. The fiberscope can also be fitted with forceps, an air jet, and a water jet for performing minor medical procedures.

The anatomy of a fiberscope

Eyepiece

Field-of-view adjustment

Angle adjustment knobs

Suction control

Air-water feed control

Water feed

Forceps opening

Air feed

Light guide

The flexible probe of this fiberscope contains a light guide for viewing. Channels running through the probe serve to introduce or suction off liquids or air; they also hold the cord to a forceps that can take tissue samples.

Forceps

Core of fiber

Cladding

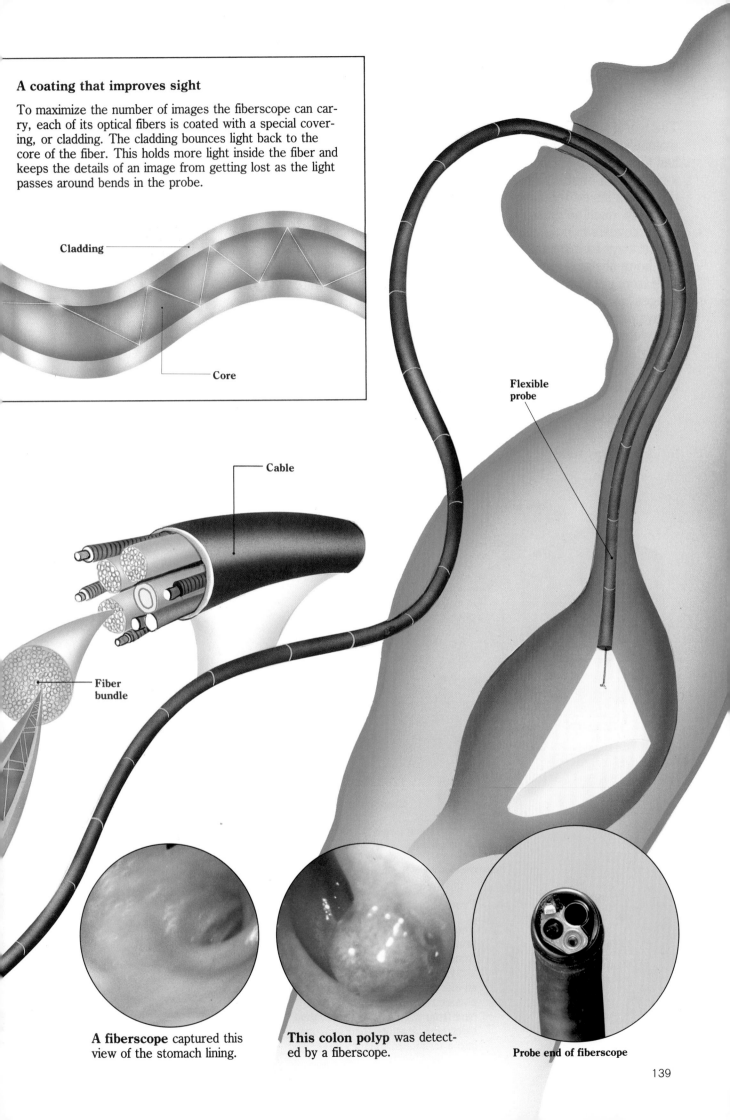

A coating that improves sight

To maximize the number of images the fiberscope can carry, each of its optical fibers is coated with a special covering, or cladding. The cladding bounces light back to the core of the fiber. This holds more light inside the fiber and keeps the details of an image from getting lost as the light passes around bends in the probe.

Cladding

Core

Cable

Fiber bundle

Flexible probe

A fiberscope captured this view of the stomach lining.

This colon polyp was detected by a fiberscope.

Probe end of fiberscope

Why Do Bones Show Up on X-Rays?

The world's first radiograph, or x-ray, showed the bones of a woman's hand. German physicist Wilhelm Roentgen *(right)* had found that by placing his wife's hand between a source of x-rays and a photographic plate, he could obtain a picture of the bones inside the hand. Yet other elements of the hand's anatomy, such as muscles, barely showed up at all. A radiograph reveals bone structure because x-rays respond in different ways to materials of different densities. Dense matter like bone absorbs most of the x-rays that hit it, keeping the rays from imprinting the film. These regions appear as white images on the radiograph. Gray to black areas form where x-rays darken the film after passing partly or entirely through lightweight matter like tissue. X-ray machines consist of an x-ray tube *(below)* and a device for positioning photographic plates. A window in the tube's housing emits a thin beam, which passes through the object being x-rayed to the film.

German physicist Wilhelm Roentgen discovered x-rays by accident in 1895 when photographic plates left near an electrified vacuum tube became fogged.

Inside an x-ray tube

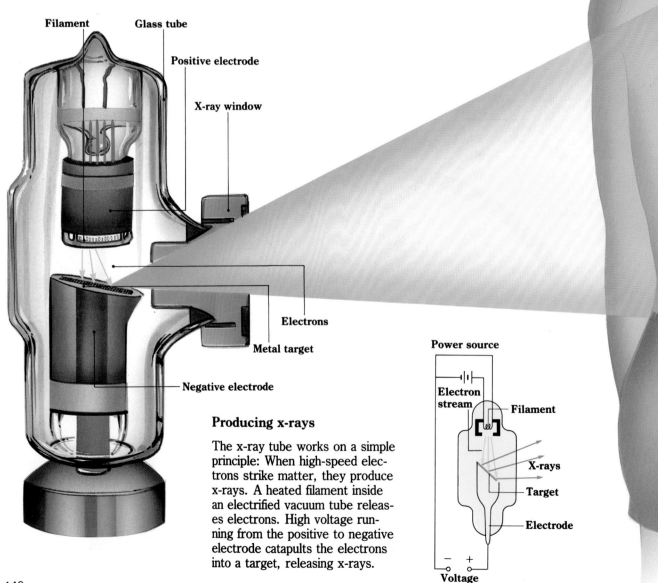

Filament

Glass tube

Positive electrode

X-ray window

Electrons

Metal target

Negative electrode

Power source

Electron stream

Filament

X-rays

Target

Electrode

Voltage

Producing x-rays

The x-ray tube works on a simple principle: When high-speed electrons strike matter, they produce x-rays. A heated filament inside an electrified vacuum tube releases electrons. High voltage running from the positive to negative electrode catapults the electrons into a target, releasing x-rays.

Pictures by degree

The ease with which x-rays pass through an object depends on the object's density. Because of this, radiographs, or x-ray pictures, record the degree to which x-rays penetrate different parts of the body. Bone, the densest material in the body, absorbs most x-rays; it therefore casts the whitest shadows on the x-ray film. Skin, muscles, and many organs have a density closer to that of water; they appear only as fuzzy tracings. The air-filled lungs allow x-rays to stream through them largely unchecked; as a result, their outline is barely discernible.

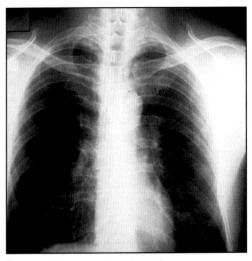

Bones show up best in a chest x-ray.

Putting x-rays in place

X-rays are one type of an invisible form of the light energy known as electromagnetic radiation. Among the various types of radiation *(right),* only gamma rays have shorter wavelengths and higher energies than x-rays. This accounts for many of the special properties of x-rays, such as their ability to penetrate solid objects. X-rays can also cause changes in the energy state of electrons in the atoms they strike, causing them to emit light or even to lose electrons.

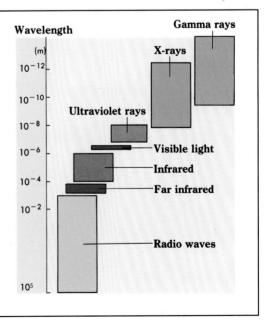

What Is a Sonogram?

Ultrasound—sound waves above the range of normal hearing—can be focused like x-rays to reveal hidden structures in the human body. Whereas ordinary sound waves flow around objects, ultrasonic waves bounce off them, forming echoes. A machine known as an ultrasonic scanner can assemble these echoes into an image, or sonogram, of the body's interior. It accomplishes this feat thanks to a transducer, a device that emits ultrasonic waves and converts their echoes into electronic signals. The ultrasound technique is used most often to observe unborn babies. One specialized apparatus, a Doppler-shift scanner, can even monitor the fetus's heart. The instrument trains an ultrasonic beam on the womb, then tracks the frequency change in the echo as the sound waves rebound off the beating heart and circulating blood.

A high-tech pulse taker

A transducer monitors fetal heartbeat by directing an ultrasonic beam at the unborn child. Moving particles in the baby's blood reflect the waves, causing measurable shifts in the echo frequencies of the waves. A computer translates these shifts into a heart rhythm.

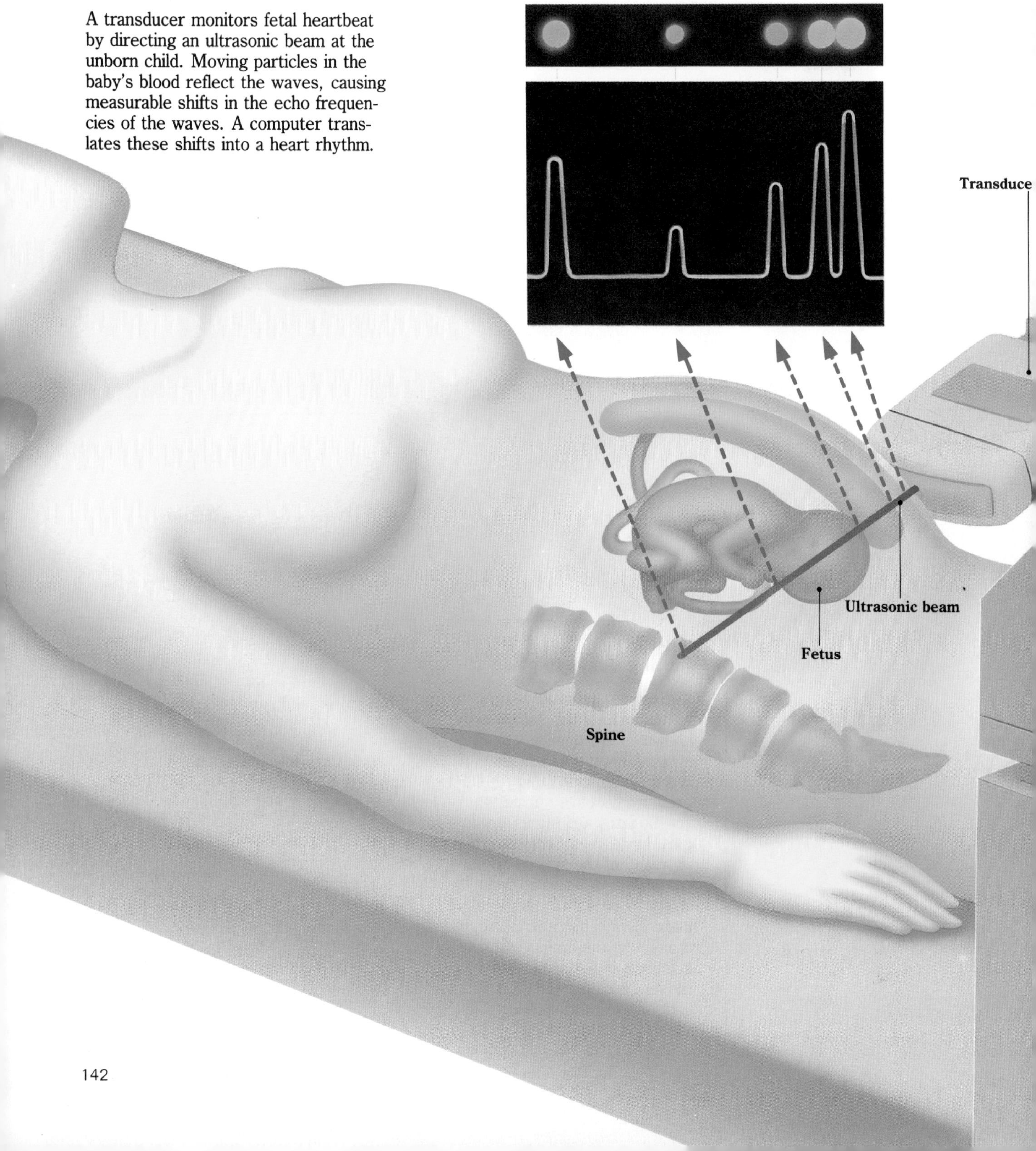

Transduce

Ultrasonic beam

Fetus

Spine

A sidelong glance

Short bursts of ultrasound yield cross-sectional images of the human body. At right, a moving transducer sends ultrasound pulses into the uterus of a pregnant woman. Pulses that hit the fetus and spine rebound as echoes. A computer logs the intensity of each pulse and the timing and direction of its echo. From these data, it calculates the location and depth of each echo-producing object, then shows them on the monitor as bright dots *(far right)*.

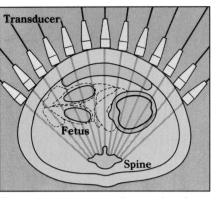

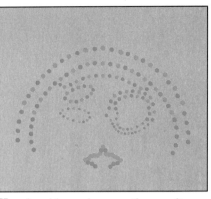

Transducer moves after each pulse.   **Head** and legs show on the monitor.

Using sound to see

Ultrasonic echo readings are converted into electronic signals that form a video image of the fetus *(right)*. Unlike x-rays, whose high energies can be harmful, ultrasonic waves produce harmless mechanical vibrations; for this reason, they are ideal for prenatal monitoring.

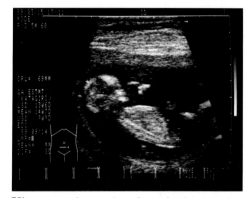

Ultrasound reveals a fetus in the womb.

Video monitor

Control panel

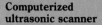

Computerized ultrasonic scanner

Why Is a Stethoscope Useful?

Before the invention of the stethoscope in 1816, doctors listened to the rhythms of the heart by pressing an ear to the patient's chest. But air between the ear and chest muffled the faint tap of the heart valves as they snapped shut, making an effective examination extremely difficult.

The modern stethoscope eliminates the sound distortion caused by air. It also suppresses external noise. Flexible rubber tubing links two snug-fitting earpieces to a chest monitor that amplifies and transmits heart and lung sounds.

The chest monitor typically has two sides. On one side is a shallow, rubber-rimmed bell for capturing low-frequency tones; on the other side is a saucerlike diaphragm that isolates sounds of higher frequency. This type of monitor enables a doctor to hear a broad range of sounds. The stethoscope is therefore a key tool for diagnosing abnormal heart conditions.

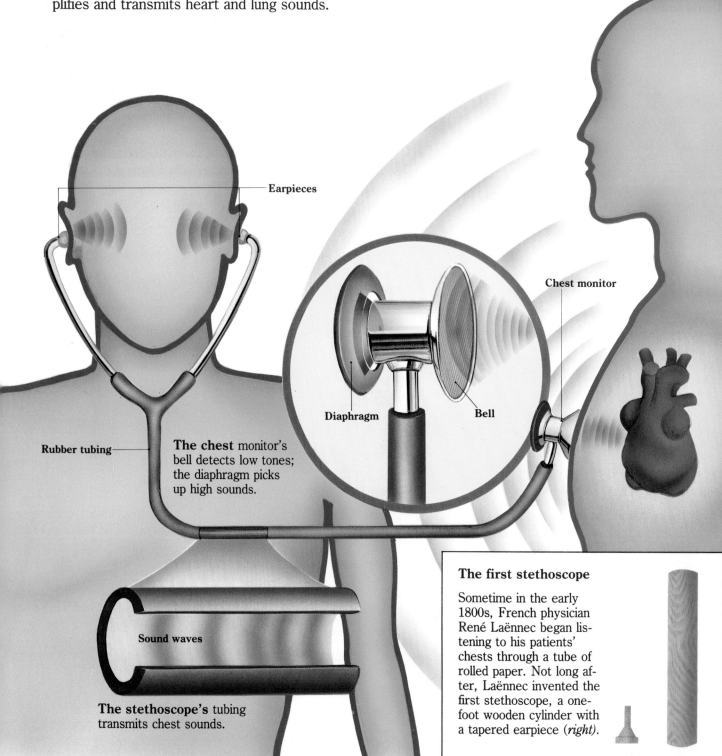

Earpieces

Chest monitor

Diaphragm

Bell

Rubber tubing

The chest monitor's bell detects low tones; the diaphragm picks up high sounds.

Sound waves

The stethoscope's tubing transmits chest sounds.

The first stethoscope

Sometime in the early 1800s, French physician René Laënnec began listening to his patients' chests through a tube of rolled paper. Not long after, Laënnec invented the first stethoscope, a one-foot wooden cylinder with a tapered earpiece (*right*).

Glossary

Accumulator: A device for storing hot fluids before they are converted to steam.

Aileron: A movable surface at the edge of a wing that controls the roll of an airplane or rocket.

Amplitude: The height of a wave.

Analog data: Information that is represented by a continuous wave or voltage.

Analog/digital (A/D) converter: A device that breaks continuous analog data signals into a string of digital data signals.

Anode: The electrode in an electron tube that attracts electrons, usually collecting and storing them.

Antimony: A metal often used in alloys.

Anvil: The fixed jaw in a micrometer.

Aperture: The opening in a camera that admits light.

Atom: The smallest particle of an element that still retains the chemical properties of that element.

Attenuation: A gradual decrease in the amplitude of an electronic signal.

Ballistic trajectory: The path of an unpowered projectile.

Binary code: A number system using two as its base that expresses numbers as strings of zeros and ones.

Bleeder valve: An opening for draining a tank or a tube.

Calipers: A measuring device consisting of two adjustable jaws.

Cam: An irregularly shaped disk whose motion gives parts in contact with it a specific rocking action.

Capacitor: A device for accumulating and holding an electric charge.

Cathode: The electron-emitting electrode of an electron tube.

Cathode-ray tube (CRT): A vacuum tube generating a focused beam of electrons, called a cathode ray.

Central processing unit (CPU): The part of a computer that interprets and executes programs.

Charge: An amount of electrical energy caused by an excess or deficiency of electrons in an atom, either positive or negative.

Charge-coupled device (CCD): A semiconductor chip equipped with light sensors that convert images into electrical signals.

Circuit breaker: A switch that automatically interrupts an electric circuit when it detects abnormal conditions.

Clutch and gearbox: A system that engages and disengages the motor of a machine, controlling the amount of power that reaches the machine.

Combustion chamber: A chamber in an engine where a mixture of fuel and oxygen is ignited to power the engine.

Commutator: A device for reversing the direction of an electric current.

Compressor: The part of a cooling system in which a pump compresses the coolant, in its gaseous state, to heat it.

Concave: Rounded inward, like the inside of a bowl.

Condensation: The process in which a gas changes into a solid or liquid.

Condenser: In optics, a lens that concentrates light. In a cooling system, the part in which the coolant releases heat and turns from a gas into a liquid.

Conductivity: The ability to transmit an electric current.

Conduit: A pipe or a tube.

Contact: A junction of electrical conductors through which an electric current passes.

Convex: Rounded outward, like the outer surface of a sphere.

Core: The ferromagnetic material that forms the central part of an electromagnet.

Deadweight valve: An opening in a pressure cooker blocked by an inert weight that is lifted by steam.

Deflection coil: A coil through which electric current is passed, creating a magnetic field that controls the beam of electrons in a television picture tube.

Diaphragm: A thin membrane or disk that divides or limits a cavity and often vibrates in response to stimuli, such as sound.

Diastole: The normal, rhythmic expansion of the heart during which its chambers fill with blood.

Digital data: Information that can be represented by a series of stepped, well-defined values.

Diode: A device that allows current to flow through a circuit in only one direction.

Electrode: A conductor through which an electric current enters or leaves a nonmetallic medium.

Electrodermal: Relating to the electrical properties of the skin.

Electromotive force: The force that causes electricity to move along a circuit to form a current; its strength is measured in volts.

Electron: An elementary particle that orbits the nucleus of an atom and has a negative electric charge.

Electron tube: A device consisting of a sealed bulb with two electrodes, between which electrons are conducted through a vacuum or gas.

Emulsion: A mixture of light-sensitive chemicals and gelatin, applied in a thin layer to photographic film or plates.

Escapement: A device in a clock that controls the speed of the wheels by allowing one tooth of a notched wheel to escape from a pallet at regular intervals. Deadbeat and verge escapements are types of pallets.

Evaporation: The process that converts a liquid or solid to a vapor or gas.

Evaporator: The part of a cooling system in which the coolant absorbs heat and changes from a liquid to a gas.

Ferromagnetic material: Any material, such as iron, that can be magnetized.

Fiber optics: Thin fibers of glass or plastic used to transmit data or images via pulses of light reflected along the fibers.

Filament: A conductive wire that glows when an electric current passes through it. In an electron tube, it acts as a cathode.

Fixer: A chemical that makes a photograph's image permanent by removing excess light-sensitive chemicals from its surface.

Flux: The dynamic flow of an electric or magnetic current.

Freon: A trade name for a variety of gases and liquid fluorocarbons used chiefly as coolants.

Frequency: The number of wave crests in a moving wave, such as a radio wave, that pass a given point per second.

Frisket: A mask of paper set in the frame of a printing press to prevent soiling of the document being printed.

Fulcrum: The support on which a lever turns.

Galley tray: A long, narrow tray used to hold set type.

Galvanometer: An instrument for detecting the existence and strength of electric current.

Gamma ray: The most energetic form of electromagnetic radiation with the highest frequency and the shortest wavelength.

Ground: An object that makes an electrical connection between an electric circuit and the earth or some other conducting body.

Gutta-percha: A tough plastic substance that resembles rubber.

Gyroaccelerometer: A device, stabilized by a gyroscope, for measuring the speed of an aircraft.

Gyrocompass: A navigational compass, made with a gyroscope, that indicates true north along the earth's surface.

Gyropilot: An electronic control system that maintains an aircraft's set heading; also called the automatic pilot.

Gyroscope: A device that rotates in all directions to maintain the same absolute direction in space in spite of the movement of its mountings.

Hertz (Hz): A unit of frequency equal to one cycle per second, used to measure radio waves. One kilohertz (kHz) is equal to 1,000 cycles per second.

Impeller: The blade of a rotor, used to transmit motion.

Induction: The process in which a body having electric or magnetic properties produces electricity, magnetism, or electromotive force in a nearby body without touching it. A current generated this way is said to be "induced."

Inertial guidance: A rocket's in-flight guidance by self-contained, automatic devices following a programmed flight path.

Integral accelerometer: An instrument that combines three gyroaccelerometers to measure acceleration in three perpendicular directions to determine a vehicle's course.

Integrated circuit (IC): A large number of tiny, interconnected electronic circuits produced on a single silicon microchip.

Interference: The property of light by which light waves strengthen or cancel each other when they meet.

Ion: An atom or molecule that has either lost or gained electrons and is electrically charged; also a free electron.

Irradiation: The process of exposing an object to radiation such as x-rays or to radiant energy such as heat or light.

Microchip: A single chip of semiconducting material on which a number of tiny electronic circuits are produced.

Micron: A unit of length equal to one-millionth of a meter.

Microprocessor: An entire central processing unit contained on a single microchip.

Microscope: An optical instrument using lenses and electromagnetic radiation to create an enlarged image of a minute object.

Modem: An electronic device that allows computers to communicate with each other using telephone lines or fiber-optic cables.

Molecule: The smallest particle of a substance that retains its properties and consists of one or more atoms.

Optics: The science that deals with light and vision.

Pallet: A lever with projections that engage and release the escapement wheel in a clock, transmitting the impulses received from the escapement to a pendulum or balance.

Photodetector: A device that triggers an electrical signal when it detects light.

Photodiode: A semiconductor device that detects and measures pulses of light by turning them into electronic signals.

Photoelectric cell: A device that produces or modifies the flow of an electric current in response to light waves.

Photoelectric tube: An electron tube with a photosensitive cathode, used like a photoelectric cell.

Photosensitive: Readily affected by light or similar radiation, such as x-rays.

Piezoelectricity: The electric current or electric polarity produced by some nonconducting crystals when under pressure.

Pinion: A small gear designed to mesh with a larger gear.

Piston: A disk or cylinder that is moved by fluid pressure, or that moves fluid, within a tightly fitting sheath.

Pitch: The distance between two adjacent screw threads; also the tilting of an aircraft's nose up or down.

Pixel: Any of the thousands of small, discrete elements that form the picture on a computer or television screen.

Pneumatic tube: A tube that is filled with air.

Pole: One of two opposite regions in an electric or magnetized body, designated positive and negative.

Polyurethane: A manmade chemical mixture similar to rubber.

Prism: A transparent body used to deviate a beam of light or to disperse it into its component colors.

Rack: A bar with teeth on one side that engages with a pinion to convert linear motion into rotary motion or vice versa.

Reed: A thin, flexible piece of cane or metal that vibrates when struck with an air current to produce sound waves.

Resistor: A device that blocks the flow of electric current moving through a circuit.

Rotor: The rotating part of a machine, often having blades.

Rudder: A vertical control surface attached to the rear of an aircraft or a boat and used to steer.

Semiconductor: Any material that can conduct electricity at high temperatures and block it at low temperatures.

Sensor: A device designed to detect a specific stimulus, such as radar waves, light, motion, or changes in temperature.

Shutter: A device that opens and closes the aperture of a camera to expose the film.

Silicon: A nonmetallic, semiconducting element from which microchips are made.

Silicone: A chemical compound made with silicon and one or more other substances.

Spindle: A rod that rotates.

Sprocket: A toothed wheel that engages a series of holes in an object, such as motion picture film, to move it along.

Stylus: A needle used to cut the grooves in making a phonograph recording; a needle used to play the recording on a phonograph.

Synchronous motor: An electric motor that runs at a speed strictly proportional to the frequency of the operating current.

Systole: The normal, rhythmic contraction of the heart during which the blood is forced out of its chambers.

Tailings: The residue and unthreshed heads of grain.

Thermal: Relating to heat or temperature.

Thermistor: A resistor whose ability to block electric current varies with temperature.

Thimble: A movable ring or tube.

Turbine: A machine having a rotor with blades, driven by the force of a moving fluid such as steam, water, or air.

Turbo pump: A pump that uses a turbine to feed fuel to a rocket engine.

Ultrasound: Sound waves with a frequency above the range of human hearing.

Venturi tube: A tube with wide ends and a narrow middle section, used to measure fluid flow by creating a difference in pressure between one end of the tube and the other.

Vernier: A scale that slides along a fixed graduated scale to indicate a fractional part of the gradations on the fixed scale.

Virtual image: An image formed by a lens or mirror.

Voltage: The force exerted in accelerating electrons along a circuit to form a current, expressed in volts.

Watt: A measurement of the amount of power yielded by a specific amount of current at a specific voltage.

Wavelength: The distance between consecutive crests of a wave.

Wave train: A succession of similar waves at regular intervals.

X-ray: High-energy radiation lying between gamma rays and ultraviolet radiation in the electromagnetic spectrum.

Yaw: The erratic movement of an aircraft in which the nose and tail swing from side to side.

Index

Staff for
UNDERSTANDING SCIENCE & NATURE

Assistant Managing Editor: Patricia Daniels
Editorial Directors: Allan Fallow, Karin Kinney
Assistant Editor/Research: Elizabeth Thompson
Editorial Assistant: Marike van der Veen
Production Manager: Marlene Zack
Copyeditors: Barbara Fairchild Quarmby (Chief), Donna Carey,
    Heidi A. Fritschel, Anthony K. Pordes
Picture Coordinator: David A. Herod
Production: Celia Beattie
Library: Louise D. Forstall
Computer Composition: Deborah G. Tait (Manager),
    Monika D. Thayer, Janet Barnes Syring, Lillian Daniels

Special Contributors, Text: Margery duMond, Barbara Mallen,
    Gina Maranto, Mark Washburn
Research: Eugenia Scharf, Lauren V. Scharf
Design /Illustration: Antonio Alcalá, Nicholas Fasciano,
    David Neal Wiseman
Photography /Illustration: Cover: Art by Stephen R. Wagner.
    1: Michael Melford/The Image Bank. 20: Photo courtesy U.S.
    Department of the Interior, National Park Service, Edison
    National Historic Site, West Orange, N. J. 22: Photo courtesy
    Thomson Consumer Electronic/RCA. Indianapolis. 49: Art by
    Al Kettler (lower right). 84: Art by Stephen R. Wagner.
Index: Barbara L. Klein
Acknowledgments: Bernard Finn, Stan Nelson, and Tom Tearman,
National Museum of American History, Smithsonian Institution
Consultant:
    Jon Eklund is curator of Physical Sciences and Computers and
    Information Technology at the National Museum of American
    History, Smithsonian Institution, Washington, D.C.

Library of Congress Cataloging-in-Publication Data
Machines & inventions.
        p.   cm. — (Understanding science & nature.)
    Includes index.
    Summary: Questions and answers introduce the biology,
habitats, and behavior of aquatic animals, from luminous fish
to fur seals.
    ISBN 0-8094-9704-2 (trade) — ISBN 0-8094-9705-0 (lib. bdg.)
    1. Machinery—Juvenile literature.
    2. Inventions—Juvenile literature.
    I. Time-Life Books.   II. Title: Machines and inventions.
    III. Series.
TJ147.M22 1993
621.8—dc20   92-35710
                                              CIP
                                              AC

TIME-LIFE for CHILDREN ™

Publisher: Robert H. Smith
Associate Publisher and Managing Editor: Neil Kagan
Assistant Managing Editors: Patricia Daniels, Elizabeth Ward
Editorial Directors: Jean Burke Crawford, Allan Fallow,
    Karin Kinney, Sara Mark
Director of Marketing: Margaret Mooney
Product Managers: Cassandra Ford, Amy Haworth,
    Shelley L. Schimkus
Director of Finance: Lisa Peterson
Administrative Assistant: Barbara A. Jones

Original English translation by International Editorial Services Inc./
C. E. Berry

Printed in Malaysia.
Published simultaneously in Canada.
Time Life Inc. is a wholly owned subsidiary of
THE TIME INC. BOOK COMPANY.
TIME LIFE is a trademark of Time Warner Inc. U.S.A.
For subscription information, call 1-800-621-7026.